The Individual
and His
Orthodox Church

The Individual and His Orthodox Church

Rev. Nicon D. Patrinacos
M.A., D. Phil. (Oxon.)

THE ORTHODOX OBSERVER PRESS

Published by:

THE ORTHODOX OBSERVER PRESS
8 East 79th St., New York, N.Y. 10021

Printed in U.S.A.

by: The Guinn Company Inc.
New York, New York

iv

Contents

Introduction

This book has been written with a particular segment of our Orthodox congregations in mind; the American born. Orthodox men and women who now comprise the bulk and make up the strength of the Orthodox parish in the new world. Predominantly, these are the people we loosely call professional, that is, experts offering specialized services either as employees or self-employed.

Few of the original business establishments of their immigrant fathers or grandfathers have survived to the present generation. Responsible for this intellectual trend (as opposed to a trade or business orientation) has been the more or less prevalent practice among the Orthodox to seek their livelihood in pursuits requiring scientific or theoretical training; perhaps this is a result of the earnest desire of the immigrant parent to equip his children with the training that would assure them a place in the American society which he proved unable to achieve for himself.

As a result of this intellect-oriented trend within the Orthodox ethnic groups, the Orthodox Church is faced with the problem of giving a convincing account of her beliefs and practices to this class of men and women who are Orthodox by baptism and outward conformity but scarcely so by inward choice. This is a result of their Church having failed — for no fault of her own — to provide them not only with an acceptable rationale of what priests say and do in church, but with an effectively organized defense against scientific and technological rationalism that is now taking the Church to the unprecedented task of fighting for her life.

This unpreparedness notwithstanding, it will be this generation of the American born Orthodox with whom the Church will survive or degenerate into small fanatical groups at variance with one another and with genuine Orthodoxy. Therefore, a correct appraising of our situation at this time together with taking the right steps for bringing our ecclesiastical atmosphere to a satisfactory degree of purity and clarity, are projects of vital importance to us.

The decade we have just entered must provide us with the setting for a massive and extensive dialogue between Church and members on points that bear on all three kinds of relationships that bring believer and Church together: the religious, the ecclesiastical, the cultural.

The religious relationship should be examined for the purpose of making our people partakers of the argument and proof of the great Fathers of the Church to the effect that Christ's teaching and redemptory work are best pursued and embodied for the sake of the individual believer by the Orthodox way of thinking and living. Obviously, this kind of enlightenment will require us to assume the state of mind and to fully understand the ways of living of the people we want to confirm in the life of the Church. An argumentation from without, however sharp it might be, will do little to touch our people's inner core of personality and will fail to open for us the gate to their innermost watchtower wherefrom they survey and evaluate the worth living states of personal being. An undertaking of this kind will require us to view our beliefs and practices from their essential aspects and to introduce, on occasion and in places, changes and reforms that, without touching on the essence of our Faith, would render it personally meaningful to Orthodox congregations of the last quarter of the twentieth century.

The second point on which we should conduct a convincing dialogue with our membership is our ecclesiastical system and its age-long order. This includes organization and discipline, community and national objectives deriving from the nature and function of an organized Church, the rights and obligations of the two segments that make up the Church of Christ — clergy and laity — and their due allegiance to the Orthodox hierarchy as it has been crystallized through the ages.

The third point issues from our Faith being also a carrier of a tradition of a cultural nature. As its dogmatical articulation was in the process of being formulated, our Faith was also impregnated with the modes of thinking and ways of living of the peoples it ushered to Orthodoxy. This mingling of belief and culture has been a subtle one, difficult to take apart, and responsibile for the particular way Orthodox parishes have grown and developed in the Americas. So, it is part of our Orthodox treasure and the substratum on which our dawning American Orthodox culture will lay its foundation and will derive therefrom its form and substance.

Then, the dialogue the Orthodox Church should conduct with her membership in the seventies cannot be limited to pure religious enlightenment; rather, it will have to examine not only the Faith in which our people have been baptized but also the ecclesiastical and cultural foundation on which Orthodoxy's baptismal font stands. And all this for the purpose of generating a personal Orthodox conscience that can congregate and aggregate into that corporate entity that renders the Church the mystical body of Christ.

Our approach is personalistic. It has been rightly pointed out that you cannot separate the individual from the group in matters of organized religion, especially the Christian religion. But the individual effects this separation himself whether the

Church approves of it or not. This, because at the present stage of human development the corporate attitude to life and its values is regulated by the degree of convergence to a common denominator of personal ingenuities and achievements. Our corporate attitude to life does not now derive from the results of a common endeavor as if today's group had a personality of its own in the nature of that of the city-state society of ancient Greece. The achievements of the group are only figuratively so while in truth they are the achievements of individuals dealing with life in a very personal way. Our approach to life is fully personalistic and unless we are completely satisfied with something, we have the option to take it or leave it.

With religion, this personal approach can prove fatal for the Church if she is not prepared to show to the individual her value and worth for him as an experience of a higher order. Our Orthodox writers should begin, then, to think about our congregations in terms of individuals instead of in terms of a flock. Our people here are certainly an aggregate of infinitely varying individuals whose personal religion can assume an equally infinite number of inward personality states and attributes. It is for all this that we should place the individual in the front row and when we take him for a tour of our Faith we should take him not only through the nave but through the altar as well.

Our other reason for selecting the phases of Orthodox teaching and practice that we have selected is that this personalistic attitude — very obvious on the community level — requires a definite and lucid articulation of our Faith on the strength of which people can recognize one another as Orthodox, as Christians deriving from the same religious climate and guarding in their hearts the same kind of divine thesaurus.

Mention was made before of the fact that the American born Orthodox congregation abounds, disproportionately to their numbers, in people with a higher academic background.

But professional people, whether they work for others or for themselves, are bound to seek the best conditions not only within their own state but within the nation as a whole. The neighborhood Orthodox parish is gradually giving way to a mobile congregation that can hardly establish itself in one place — at least in so far as its more or less elite segment is concerned. And where there is no appreciable movement of the professional element, the group that has done well in one place moves to a better neighborhood or another city. Moving from one city to another and from one state to another are not rare occurrences any more with our Orthodox congregations.

When the Orthodox finds himself in a new locale, in all but the most irreligious cases, he will seek his Church. But meeting new people becomes more rewarding if the acquaintance has a common ground from which to spring and grow into friendship. National origin begins to fade out among the Orthodox as a strong binding force for social communication and establishment of productive friendships. It seems that religious identification will remain one of the strongest forces that will bring people together. But in order to bring out and share the element of identity in an acquaintance, people have to communicate by way and on the strentgh of this identical characteristic. Orthodox people have had hardly anything in the nature of essential beliefs and practices that they could use as emotional and spiritual binders between them.

This book aims at providing the Orthodox with some of the most outstandingly characteristic beliefs and practices of the Orthodox Church which concern the individual personally and to which he can refer as experiences of a higher order on which communication of minds and hearts can be effected. It is only this communication of minds and hearts, effected on the strength of beliefs and practices of a personal nature, that can bind the Orthodox together; not, as in the past, theological differentiations from other Christians and, definitely, not the sharing of hatred against other Churches.

We are aiming, then, at providing a spiritual and rational common denominator by which the new membership of the Orthodox Church can identify themselves on both the parish and inter-parish levels. But this identification will not be effected on the strength of the mere knowledge of these characteristic beliefs and practices but on the people's acceptance of them as being rationally defensible and as referring to situations of life that are within the circumference of their own experience, specific to our Church but not spiritually and culturally strange to the point of invoking avoidance.

Our last chapter, Facing the Present and the Future, will, no doubt, surprise some and sour the disposition of others from among our traditional theologians who have been contented to play the same theological record for ten centuries now. But meanwhile our Orthodoxy was manhandled by both race and nation, enriched outwardly but, in many respects, impoverished inwardly. This acculturation constitutes part of our Orthodox heritage today, and our handling of it will in large measure decide the survival or not of our Church here. One of the outcomes of our Orthodox acculturation through time and different peoples is our imperative need now for a liturgical reform for the purpose of rendering Orthodox worship meaningful and effective to our people today.

This little book could claim the honor of being the first examination of Orthodoxy, in any language, from a true to name personal viewpoint, as well as being the first anatomical delving in it from the viewpoint of the social sciences. Should it succeed to even disturb our age-long conviction of institutional and theological adequacy, its purpose will have been fulfilled; our people will be given a fresh start in the life in Christ and in the life of the Church.

N. D. P.

I

The Sacraments

The Greek name for sacrament is *mysterion*, a term unlike the Latin *ministerium* or mistery, and different in meaning from the Hellenistic *mystery*, the latter denoting a secret or puzzling experience. The Latin *ministerium* denotes a craft or a guild, hence Mystery Plays were the plays performed by trade-guilds.

The Greek *mysterion* was a rite which was kept secret from those who were not properly prepared to witness it and profit personally from its performance. The name *mysterion* comes from the verb *myein* which means to shut the mouth or eyes for the purpose of preventing revelation of things seen or heard to all save those who were properly prepared. The officer who by right of some extraordinary privilege was entrusted with revealing the secret to those properly prepared, and so with initiating them to the mystery, was called *Hierophantes*, the revealer of holy things, whose equivalent in a remote way is the priest of the Christian sacraments. Although in essence the Greek mysteries are, obviously, fundamentally unlike the Christian sacraments, their outward ritual does not seem to be as extensively unlike our own sacramental practices.

Christian thought and practice were markedly influenced by Greek philosophy and religion, especially by ideas and practices that seemed to entertain a mystical trend aimed at bringing man closer to God by way of metaphysical meditation or ritualistic practice. Neoplatonism, among other philosophico-religious trends exerted a really deep influence on the development of Christianity in both East and West. Yet, as we shall clearly indicate in some detail later on, the Christian sacraments stand unique in the history of religion as regards their underlying ideas and, above all, as regards the relationship between man and God they imply.

Primitive Church mysteries were considered to be situations or sayings which bore an essential connection with the one supreme mystery in the experience of the Christian, the mystery of the Incarnation and the drama that followed God's taking the human flesh in the person of Christ. These mysteries were either objects of symbolic significance, such as the Cross, or sayings used for teaching the believers, such as the mystery of the Trinity, and all other beliefs of the Christians which could not be accounted for by reason. According to the primitive Church, behind these mysteries there stood the Grace of Christ by which things visible as well as invisible had been brought about for the benefit of man.

Gradually, though, as the individual grew more and more in want of tangible means of union with Christ, the mysteries of the primitive Church — being in the main symbols and teachings — became ceremonies for the purpose of not only symbolizing the great mystery of salvation but for sanctifying the individual with the Grace of the Spirit of Christ.

Baptism is the first Christian ceremony which was performed not symbolically but actually for the purpose of santifying the individual by washing out his sins and by filling him with the Grace of the Spirit. And since Christ was considered to be both the source of Grace and the actual founder of these ceremonies, the Christian sacraments gradually grew to mean "certain divinely instituted ceremonies by which the Grace of Christ is imparted to the believers." Therefore, one can view the sacraments from three aspects: the fact of their being divinely instituted, their outward expression in terms of ceremonial procedure, and the nature of the imparted Grace.

Christ and our Sacraments

The belief by which Christ has been the direct or indirect founder of the sacraments appears to be universally current in the Apostolic and sub-Apostolic periods. New Testament writers are explicit in stating that the Grace of God had been realized in Jesus Christ and by Jesus Christ, and the Apostles, in their role as successors to the work of Christ, did everything in the name and by the authority of Christ.

Two of those Grace imparting ceremonies, Baptism and Eucharist, were founded directly by Christ and by a straightforward command to the Apostles. Although the rest of the sacraments cannot be substantiated on the strength of Biblical evidence to have been directly commanded by Christ, there is no evidence to suggest that they are the invention of the Apostles.

3

The Apostles could not have agreed on such important additions to the ritual and life of the primitive Church had they not been conscious of acting not only in the name but also on the authority of Christ. The fact that the ceremonial core of that which later developed into a more elaborate ritual was performed by the Apostles in the name of Christ stands as indirect but extremely significant evidence to the fact that the Apostles considered Christ to be the founder of those acts by which man was believed to be empowered with divine strength and fortification.

Apostolic unanimity on primitive sacramental practices becomes more important considering the negative attitude which the Apostles used to adopt toward views or actions which did not meet with the approval of all twelve. This spirit of scrutiny, apparently aiming at guarding the Church against erroneous teachings from within and without, was zealously preserved by the early Church on the example of the Apostles; the element of catholicity — universality — in teachings and practices was held to be the indispensable ingredient of genuineness.

As the Apostolic period faded out in time and the Church began her turbulent development through the ages, those acts of the Apostles believed to impart the Grace for the purpose of individual sanctification continued uninterrupted and undisputed, were gradually singled out from other ceremonies, and were brought into supreme eminence in the life of the Church.

The Fathers who succeeded the Apostles in the work of preserving the *logia* (the sayings) and the spirit of Christ's teaching together with their Apostolic interpretation, are unanimously of the opinion that the power which these ceremonies impart originates from God, or from Jesus Christ, or from the Holy Spirit, or from all three persons of the Holy Trinity. The distinction between sacraments directly instituted by Christ, such as Baptism and Eucharist, and others founded by the Apostles lack Biblical or other historical support.

The belief that Christ is the founder of the sacraments should not be stressed, however, to the point of Christ Himself having arranged the mode of their performance or even their number. It appears that though Christ instituted in essence the sacraments, He left to the Apostles, under the guidance of the Spirit, the ordering of the visible part in accordance with each occasion for which the Grace of the Spirit is imparted to the individual. A striking illustration of this interpretation is the sacrament of Penance, which though instituted by Christ, was never arranged by Him in regard to performance or to situations and personality states for which the sacrament is ceremoniously performed.

A sacrament becomes the subject of human experience by virtue of words uttered and of actions performed by the celebrant in the presence of a body of believers. These words and actions constitute the experiential garment of the sacrament while the imparting of Grace — believed to take place at some point during the utterance of words and the performing of actions — constitutes the invisible or transcendental part of the sacrament.

The relationship between the outward manifestations of the sacrament and the invisible core, the Grace, has been the subject of much theological discussion and dispute. The question has been asked: are the words and actions of the celebrant inseparably connected with the imparting of the

Grace in such a manner as to have the Grace imparted whenever certain words are uttered and certain actions are performed irrespective of any other factor? That means, does the imparting of Grace depend upon the utterance of specific words and upon specific actions on the part of a priest? This, in turn, resolves to the most fundamental question in regard to miraculous Christianity: how does the infinite become expressed in terms of human experience and by way of the finite?

Fathers as early as Origen and Cyril of Alexandria were concerned with this question which was also minutely examined later by the Schoolmen and other theologians. Origen and his disciples spoke of the purification of the soul in Baptism irrespective of the baptismal water, while Cyril of Alexandria believes in a transubstantiation of the baptismal water into a divine and ineffable power. Both of these views have been on occasion stretched to the limits of their underlying rationale, and the result has been — as with all kinds of theological rationalism — religious magic on the one hand, or the complete separation of the infinite from the finite, on the other.

If Grace is completely conditioned by the mechanics of the sacrament, sacramental utterances accompanied by certain actions must impart the Grace as if by a magic power which those words and actions appear to possess. In the light of this interpretation, the Christian sacraments differ little from the Eleusinian mysteries in which purification was sought by such a magic imprisonment of the infinite by the finite.

If, on the other hand, Grace is considered to be completely independent of the outward part of the sacrament, the very idea of the sacrament as a performance by which the Grace is imparted to the individual is invalidated, and the very mystery of the Incarnation becomes impossible inasmuch as the infinite stands in no relationship to the finite. In practice, the Church has pursued neither of these two views to its breaking point, seeing that that which really matters is the belief that the Grace is indeed imparted to the individual provided that certain considerations and conditions have been taken into proper account.

Sacraments and Personal Salvation

The question is whether or not the sacraments are necessary for personal salvation. The Orthodox Church is of the definite belief that the sacraments are indeed necessary if the individual is to appropriate the Grace which, by Biblical definition, is the all-important means to salvation. Orthodox theologians, from the early Greek Fathers to this day, have always considered the Church of Christ to be the only instrument of personal salvation on the ground of explicit Biblical and Apostolic evidence by which the work of salvation begun by Christ continues through the Church and by the Church in her capacity as the mystical body of the Lord.

The Apostles understood the Church to be an institution in which Christ is ever-present by His Spirit for the purpose of perpetuating the work of redemption originally effected on the Cross. This perpetuation is carried on by the sacraments through which the experiential link between the historical Jesus and the individual is established in terms of personal consciousness. This Apostolic concept of the Christian Church has been kept unaltered by the Greek Fathers and has since been used as the basis on which subsequent Orthodox theology has developed.

The idea underlying the concept of the Church being the only treasury of salvation appears to be closely connected with two premises, both characteristic of Orthodoxy: the first, to the effect that Christ remains eternally with His Church in fulfilment of His promise; the second, attesting to the believed fact that the moral constitution of man needs outside support and fortification lest it forfeit the Grace.

Christ remains eternally with His Church by means of His Spirit abiding ever with the Church and by the presence of His Mystical Body in the Eucharist. Had the Church been devoid of the Holy Spirit and of the Eucharistic Body of Christ, Incarnation, Crucifixion, and Resurrection, would have remained mere historical events detached from the personal experience of all those who did not happen to witness them in time. But in that case, the religion of Christ would differ little, if any, from the other religions the founders of which left to their followers only their teachings and the historical memory of their presence among people at some time in the history of man. There are a number of such religious teachers who still light the path of many people by virtue of that which they did and that which they taught others to do, but, nonetheless, they remain among their followers only as memory images and as mere systems of thought. Christ, according to His own statement, intended to do much more for man than He would were He one of the great teachers of mankind. He intended to remain forever as mankind's ready and accessible savior by means of a redemption effected once but continually offered in the experience of man through the Grace of His Spirit. The Apostles understood Christ to be among them all the time,

8

as is evidenced by their prayers and by their teaching to the effect that Christ remains with the Church "forever and ever."

Relative to the second premise, the fact to the effect that the moral constitution of man needs outside support began to become concrete as the Christian Apologists, and later the rest of the great Fathers, were attempting to formulate an argumentative rationale on behalf of Christianity. While articulating their teachings, the Fathers were constantly confronted with the fact that man's moral constitution is fragile to a degree that would not allow a consistently moral behavior on the part of the individual irrespective of his determination to stay within the bounds of the good life. Of course, it was St. Paul who first realized that the Christian's chances to constantly adhere to the ways of an illumined life were rather slim, unless his wavering determination to defeat the desires of worldly living were fortified from outside.

This outside help was believed to be granted to the believer in the form and content of certain experiential situations by which the historical person of Christ was rendered a living experience of the individual. Baptism and Eucharist were certainly taken to be more than symbolic acts; rather, they were understood to be situations of life involving not only the individual's rational and emotional faculties but his whole personality as well. During their performance, certain physical actions take place by which the mental content of these two sacraments is translated into an experience in which the individual finds himself involved for the purpose of achieving a purely spiritual end.

It appears, then, that the true purpose of these two

sacraments of the primitive Church was to effect the mystery of the Incarnation in terms of human experience, to bring the finite man in contact and union with the infinite in terms of waking consciousness. These practices are important not only as events in personal experience prescribed by Christ, but as evidence of the intent of Christ to remain with man forever through His Grace by which alone the individual is helped realistically and effectively toward his desired salvation.

Man was believed to be unable to effectively appropriate the redemption which issued from the Cross. The Patristic argument was to the effect that man is easily distracted from his spiritual goals, he is too fragile to stand firm against his material desires and hardly able to effect in himself the life in Christ without the aid of the Church and without the Grace that renders the Church the living body of Christ. Apostolic alertness and constant preparedness against the eventuality of relapsing into un-Christian life underlie the belief that man has been saved potentially but not independently of his will and of his ability to keep himself in the state of salvation. And though the redemption of man has been the work of God, one's salvation is still one's own concern for which, however, the individual must receive help from outside his willing powers.

If salvation were an affair between man and God only, an act of mental acquiescence to the events and meaning of Christ's life would probably suffice to keep the individual in the state of salvation forever. But since Christianity is more a way of life than a philosophical viewing of life, it involves the willing powers of man rather than his mental and emotional attitudes and, as such, it finally resolves into a person to person relationship which, in turn, determines the individual's relationship to God.

Thus viewed, the sacraments have to be considered indispensable to personal salvation inasmuch as membership in the Church of Christ is indispensable to being one of Christ. Accordingly, Orthodox theologians are of the definite belief that every true member of the Church must partake of the sacraments through which the Grace aids the individual in keeping his ties with Christ unbroken and in furthering in himself the development of the life in Christ.

Not all of the sacraments are obligatory to every Orthodox. The Grace imparted to the individual in each sacrament differs in nature according to the situation of life to which it applies. By the sacrament of Baptism, one is justified in the sense that both the original sin and one's own personal transgressions are cleansed, and the new life in Christ is subsequently sealed by the sacrament of Confirmation. By Eucharist, the individual is supplied with eternal spiritual food by way of the Body and Blood of Christ, while by the sacraments of Penance and Unction one is redeemed from sins subsequent to baptism and is kept in spiritual health. By the sacrament of Priesthood, one is enabled to successfully perform the mission of bringing Christ into the lives of others, and by the sacrament of Matrimony the Christian is helped to live by the ways of God personal relationships of the most important nature to both the individual and to the Christian community at large.

The situations of life with which the sacraments deal evidently relate to the most important aspects of personal living and, as such, they are states of being for which a true

11

Christian needs the aid of the Grace. No member of the Church is required to partake of all the sacraments but only of those which apply to situations of life in which he, on occasion, finds himself and for which there is a corresponding sacrament. And though Orthodox theology has no authoritative opinion regarding instances in which one, though willing to partake of the necessary sacrament, is unable to do so because of adverse circumstances, the Orthodox teaching is emphatic in condemning individuals who, due to personal negligence or indifference, do not receive the Grace of the sacraments.

Factors Conditional to Imparting the Grace

A sacrament is validly performed and the Grace is considered to have been imparted if, first, a visible act of performance takes place. This visible performance, the celebration of the sacrament, consists of words and actions which are woven around a sacramental core for the purpose of enhancing and further explaining the meaning of that which takes place.

With the sacrament of Baptism, for example, the sacramental core is the immersing of the individual into the sanctified water in the name of the Father, and of the Son, and of the Holy Spirit. Yet the sacrament as a whole consists of a series of prayers and actions which, though in essence are only contributory to the meaning of the Biblical description of Baptism, have come to constitute an important liturgical part of the sacrament in the form of a prologue and an epilogue to this great event and to its significance for the individual.

At this point, one cannot overemphasize the belief of the Orthodox Church to the effect that the words and actions in a sacrament are not to be taken to possess a magic power in themselves; rather, they are an observable presentation of the faith of the Church on the strength of which alone the Grace is imparted to the individual.

The Grace is not imparted because of the utterance of certain words and because of the observance of certain forms by the celebrant. Those words and actions do not mechanically effect the imparting of Grace; only the living faith of the Church is responsible for it, a faith which is, in turn, expressed by the words and actions of a sacrament. This means that the faith of the Church and the performance of a sacrament are identical in the sense that the invisible faith of the Church in what is done is expressed by the audible and visible means of words and actions.

This is important, especially in relation to the baptism and other sacraments of heretics. Though a heretical baptism may appear outwardly identical with Orthodox baptism, yet it is not so inasmuch as the faith behind the words and actions is different from the Orthodox faith. An outwardly valid performance does not make a sacrament valid in a dogmatical sense unless the teaching and faith behind the observable occurrences are in complete agreement with the outward form of the sacrament.

The next question which has been earnestly debated since very early in the history of the Church is whether the faith and personal worth of the celebrant affects the validity of a sacrament and, more important, the actual imparting of the Grace. If the bishop and priest are the only ones entitled to perform a sacrament, they must — by logical necessity — be absolutely qualified spiritually and morally to perform a function in which the infinite is believed to mingle with and sanctify the finite.

It has been rightly pointed out that there can be no other event in the experience of man through which the divine makes its abode within the human by means of certain evidenced acts that are performed by one particular individual. Furthermore, since the performance of a sacrament depends in a way upon the will of the priest without whom no sacrament can be performed, the priest proves to be not only the channel through which the Grace is imparted, but an agent of God who can exercise considerable control over His Grace. The first question is, then, can the sacramental Grace be imparted through an unworthy celebrant of a sacrament?

The layman's answer was advanced a long time ago and is still held to be valid by many a Christian. The impure, according to this answer, cannot mix with the pure, and so no unworthy priest can really prove instrumental in imparting the Grace in a sacrament. This seems to be a perfectly logical answer if one assumes the priest to perform the sacraments by an unconditional personal right. In reality, however, the priest is only commissioned by the Church to perform the sacraments in the capacity of the agent of the One who is believed to be the actual celebrant of the sacraments. The right by which a priest performs the sacraments is actually a byproduct of the Grace he received with his priesthood. He has no real personal control over it, just as the Apostles had no withholding control over the mission to which they were assigned by Christ — that is, to preach the Gospel and offer salvation to those who believed and were baptized.

Just as the Apostles were merely the instruments of establishing the militant Church of Christ, so the priest is only the instrument for dispensing the Grace of Christ to the individual for the latter's moral and spiritual fortification and ultimate salvation. If we believe that the priest has an inherent right to dispense or withhold the Grace at will, Christ is no longer with the Church, and the believers—constituting as they do the mystical body of Christ — are reduced to a membership of a purely social institution. This, however, is not only contrary to both Biblical teaching and Apostolic practice, but it destroys the very nature of the Church as an institution of divine origin and nature.

The Church has always held the belief to the effect that the spiritual and moral state of the priest is inconsequential to the imparting of the Grace, and his will to perform a sacrament must be taken to be actually expressing the consciousness and faith of the Church. The faith of the Church is the primary prerequisite for the valid performance of a sacrament. The Church has consequently laid down certain conditions under which a sacrament may be performed by a priest. In this way the Church controls the extent and application of the priestly commission to perform a sacrament.

In the belief of the Church, it is Christ Himself who dispenses the Grace in a sacrament, the priest being entrusted through His Apostles only with the visible part of imparting the Grace. An Orthodox theologian once likened the priest to a water pipe through which, rusty as it may be, clear water issues. Finally, if the moral quality of the priest is considered to be conditional to the imparting of the sacramental Grace, personal sanctification resulting from sacraments would be in doubt, and the very concept of the Church as a visible communion of saints would be seriously impaired.

But if the personal faith or morality of the celebrant of a sacrament is of no consequence to the imparting of Grace, then sacraments performed by priests entertaining heretical beliefs must be just as valid as sacraments performed by an Orthodox priest. This conclusion, however logical it may appear to be, proves finally untenable because the priest, as has already been pointed out, acts on behalf of the Church and is believed to uphold her genuine faith and practice. If he believes or practices otherwise, he forfeits his commission and ceases to be the instrument of Christ in sacramental procedure, since Christ operates only through the consciousness and conscience of His true Church, that is, through the Church which abides by His true teachings as transmitted to her by His Apostles.

The Orthodox Church, firmly believing all through her long history that the Grace of the Spirit does not operate outside the Church, has condemned sacraments performed by heretics, even though they might appear to have been performed in outward conformity with genuine Orthodox practices. Both ancient and later Fathers agree with Irenaeus that, "where the Church there the Holy Spirit," and speak either directly or through Synodical canons about heretical baptisms and ordinations being completely null and void.

The Principle of Economy

This practice appears to be strange and seemingly inconsistent with the Church's customary conformity to dogmatical beliefs and Synodical edicts and directives. It has been interpreted by later Synods and Fathers, such as St. Basil, as an attitude embodying the concern of the Church not only for her own spiritual and organizational well-being but for that of her fallen members as well who seek readmission into her spiritual and institutional enclosure in which alone does the Spirit operate.

This attitude is called *economy*, a Greek term denoting conservation of spiritual, mental, and material powers and resources. The question as to when this attitude was proposed and by whom, and how the conscience of the Church first reacted to it, are historically obscure, although it appears to have been firmly established and unquestionably accepted by the Church by the time of the Nicene Council early in the fourth century.

The dogmatical foundation of this principle seems to rest on the belief that the Church, being the treasury of Grace, has the right to make exceptions to any rule for the purpose of arresting the development of evil situations within the membership of the Church of Christ. It may be that in terms of the evangelical concept of the one flock under one Shepherd, this method of compromising discordant situations within the Church is the most practical and the most Christian attitude that the Church as mother should take toward those of her dissident children who decide to return under the maternal shelter.

Nevertheless, the principle of economy appears to be

arbitrary and inconsistent with the fundamental concept of the Church being the ark and treasury of Grace. If the Church has the right to contradict herself, what does really happen to those heretical sacraments at the moment they are accepted as valid by the Church? Are they automatically validated, or are they made valid by the Church? If the latter is the case, does this mean that the Church has the power to render valid the non-valid according to circumstances?

One explanation regards the sacraments of heretics, once they are accepted by the Church, as filled with new life and in a sense spiritually vivified, like old bottles filled with new contents. However, this explanation has been rejected by the Church because it implies the existence of heretics who perform the sacraments validly, a view irreconcilable with the practice of the Church of rebaptizing some returning heretics but not others. Furthermore, such an explanation contradicts the belief of the Church to the effect that no sacrament can be validly performed outside the Church.

Another explanation focuses our attention to the rights and privileges of the Church with regard to the administration of the sacraments and to the dispensation of the Grace, rather than upon the effects on the sacraments of heretics at the time they are readmitted to the Church. According to this second explanation, the Church, being an autonomous community of believers, has absolute control over the sacraments for the purpose of implementing, with as little strife as possible, her primary aim of the salvation of the individual. Equipped with such authority, the Church simply proceeds to make valid the sacraments of those heretics whom she readmits to her membership.

In accordance with this last understanding and despite the fact that it lacks clarification as a theological tenet as well as an ecclesiastical practice, economy has been used on many occasions in the past and is still used by the Orthodox Church. Apparently, the Church is motivated by reasons superior to theological explanations and rules of logical consistency. It may be that the long overdue Eighth General Council will lay down the criteria by which the principle of economy will be applied in the future. Many Orthodox theologians find the principle of economy too loosely defined to be safely explained and adequately defended in terms of theological arguments.

On the other hand, others believe that the principle of economy was never meant by the Church to be expressed in terms of Canonical decrees, or by a set of rules to be used as authoritative guides whenever circumstances require their application. The Church has by experience found the principle of economy useful in meeting adversities which could otherwise have torn the seemless garment of Christ into even more pieces. In exercising her indisputably Apostolic authority with regard to dispensing the Grace, the Church found that her course in properly evaluating circumstances should be motivated by love rather than by conformity to rational coherence and consistence. She must have also learned that human situations, whether they concern individuals or groups, are fundamentally so irrational and inexplicable that they follow no pattern for which a rule can be devised. No two situations to which the principle has been applied in the past have been identical in either form or content. Rather, they have been unique situations requiring a unique handling lest their apparent similarities invoke rules of conformity which in reality could not apply to them. That is perhaps the reason for which the Church has not yet drawn up an inflexible rule of reference but has left the application of the economy practice to the wisdom of each local Church.

Therefore, although the fundamental beliefs of the Orthodox Church concerning her relationships with her members are irrevocable, she has been willing to pay the price of self-contradiction for the purpose of keeping within her saving reach as many individuals as possible. Who can tell what Christianity would be today had not the Nicene Council applied the principle of economy in its deliberations concerning powerful, and in most cases sincere, personalities and groups temporarily found outside the Church?

The Validity of a Sacrament

In the celebration of a sacrament two parties are immediately involved, the priest and the recipient of the sacrament. Since the celebrant priest acts as the instrument by which the Grace is transmitted, he must fulfill certain conditions before the sacrament is considered to be theologically and canonically valid. It has been already mentioned that the priest in his capacity as an instrument through which the Grace is imparted to the recipient of the sacrament, cannot dispense or withhold the Grace at will. Once a sacrament is performed according to the prescribed ceremony, the Grace is imparted to the individual for whom the sacrament has been celebrated. In other words, the priest is not in a position to dispense the Grace of a sacrament to one person and withhold it from another, even if he so wishes. The first condition, then, which must be observed by the celebrant is the performance of the sacrament according to the ritual prescribed by the Church.

The second condition without which no sacrament is considered to be valid either theologically or canonically, is the will of the priest to perform the sacrament. This means that the priest must proceed to celebrate a sacrament freely and without compulsion from without, fully knowing and realizing that which he is doing.

His control over dispensing or withholding the sacramental Grace is, then, physical rather than spiritual. Once he proceeds to celebrate a sacrament free of physical or mental duress, the spiritual aspect of that which he does— if he does it correctly — is beyond the control of his personal intentions or his will. If the spiritual aspect of a sacrament were conditional to the personal will of the priest, doubt and confusion would result as to which sacraments were validly performed and which not, and the Church would by necessity forfeit her absolute control over the sacraments to the priest's personal intentions.

With the celebration of the sacrament on the part of the priest, the intention of the Church to dispense the Grace for the purpose of the individual's salvation is carried out to its logical and natural conclusion. From this point on, it is the recipient of the sacrament himself who has to see that the received Grace becomes operative in him and finally results in his personal salvation.

We must, then, distinguish between the intent of a sacrament and its effectiveness in the soul of the recipient. This distinction was made by St. Paul: "He who eateth and drinketh unworthily, eateth and drinketh damnation to himself, not discerning the Lord's body and blood." Responsible for effacing the sins of the recipient of a sacrament is Christ, or the Holy Spirit, but the individual himself can block the operation of the Grace by being unprepared to receive the gift of the Spirit, or by antagonizing its operation through lack of faith or Godless ways of life. The proper preparation for receiving the Grace of a sacrament has always been considered to consist of faith in God and His redemptory work for man through Christ, of the admission of one's sinful status, and finally of an earnest and sincere desire to be saved.

The belief by which the sacraments work in man by themselves and irrespective of the individual's inner disposition and will to be saved, is not consistent with the meaning of so many situations presented by Christ Himself. The kingdom of God is likened to a banquet to which many are invited but few attend, and the Word of God bears fruits only if it falls upon fertile ground. The belief of the Orthodox Church that the sacraments operate in man after proper preparation and only with his whole-hearted cooperation is in accord with the whole Christian philosophy of man by which the individual retains his own free will even after he has been offered salvation by Christ.

Why Seven Sacraments?

The sacraments are seven: Baptism, Chrism (Confirmation), Confession (Penance), Communion (Eucharist), Priesthood, Marriage (Matrimony), and Unction. A question which has on occasion intrigued Sunday School teachers as well as serious theologians is why are the sacraments seven and only seven. Is there Biblical or Apostolic evidence as to their number, or any other reason for which the Church has finally instituted seven ceremonies by which the Grace of the Spirit is believed to be imparted to the individual?

Various explanations have been offered for the number seven, but without really explaining it. There is no Biblical or Apostolic indication why the sacraments should be seven. Some theologians in their attempt to explain the number seven and invest it with Biblical support, have resorted to the Book of Revelation and have tried to relate the number seven — prominently figuring through this book — with the seven sacraments. Their arguments are mystical and allegorical but unconvincing, so much so that early Fathers mention in their discources two or three of the seven sacraments. St. John Chrysostom and St. Augustine mention Baptism and Eucharist as being the essential elements of the sacramental life of the Church. St. John of Damascus mentions three — Baptism, Chrism, Eucharist — and other Fathers of authority seem to agree with the number two or three.

However, the fact that the Fathers do not mention all seven sacraments does not mean that they did not know them, or that they did not take them all to be of equal validity and importance. The Fathers, and for that matter the whole Church, did not specifically state current beliefs as dogmas unless such beliefs were attacked and had to be defended. The first occasion in which the number of the sacraments had to be specifically stated did not present itself until 1274, when emperor Michael Palaeologos deposited a kind of Orthodox Confession before the Synod of Lyons.

Undoubtedly, the Fathers knew all seven sacraments as means of transmitting the Grace. Their awareness of all seven sacraments is unquestionably testified by Tradition and by early liturgical books. The Monophysites and Nestorians, separated from the Church in the fifth century, were firm believers in the seven sacraments as means of personal salvation. This is clear from their liturgical books, in which the sacrament of Baptism, as well as the other six, are found clearly distinguished from other ceremonies.

It may be that, though the content and meaning of the sacraments as means of imparting the Grace were known and believed from the very beginning, they continued to be mentioned with other liturgical acts and symbols which originally bore the name *mysterion*, as has been previously indicated. Gradually, however, the term *mysterion* was reserved for those particular ceremonies by which the Grace is imparted to man on the strength of the right of the Church to offer salvation to believers by perceptible acts and tangible means.

And yet there is no explanation why the sacraments should be seven apart from the importance of the seven situations in life to which they apply. The situations for which the sacraments are performed are situations of personal life that include the fundamental experiences in the physical, mental, and spiritual life of the individual. As such, they cover the whole field of waking life of man and constitute the groundwork upon which will and emotions build the continuum of life.

It is the teaching of the Church that the physical life of

the individual without the animation of Christian living is empty and unproductive save as far as instinctive behavior is concerned. Christian living is as important to man as physical being, for without the ways of Christian living the individual merely exists but has no opportunity to develop his talent for love by which alone he is clearly distinguishable from the rest of the animals.

The seven sacraments deal with the most important junctures of Christian living and, for that matter, with the most important junctures of life in every civilized society. By Baptism the individual is spiritually reborn, by Chrism he is confirmed in the new life, and by Eucharist he is united with Christ and given life eternal. The illnesses of the soul are cured by the sacrament of Penance, and the illnesses of the body by Unction. The sacrament of Marriage covers one of the most important stages in the development of human personality and is entrusted with the sacred end of mankind's survival in nature. The Priesthood constitutes a mission and a walk of life by which one assumes responsibility in the eyes of God not only for himself but for others as well. All seven sacraments appear to have been designed to meet situations which make life not only worth living but a superior state of being which man could never experience by means of his own mental and emotional apparatus had not Christ shifted the center of life from earth to heaven.

There is a final question which is constantly asked by individuals who believe that even divine situations must yield an explanation in terms of rational understanding and logical measurements: is Grace really transmitted in the sacraments? Many answers have been advanced to this question, some on the basis of textual evidence and others on the basis of theological arguments. One of those simpler individuals who live their religion rather than think it out said that whether or not the Grace of God is transmitted in the sacraments is a matter for the individual to discover. The individual has to find out for himself — as is the rule of life with all situations that really matter in personal living. Those who have reached conclusions of their own, he said, state that the way of discovery is the way of faith which has proven to be the only means by which the incognizable is ultimately understood and known.

Orthodox Sacraments and Greek Mysteries

The suggestion that the Orthodox sacraments are little more than copies of pagan mysteries is, to say the least, uncritical considering that fundamental differences between a pagan mystery and an Orthodox sacrament are too obvious to be overlooked — to say nothing of the fact that scholars know comparatively little of the ritual of the Greek mysteries and are thus unable to draw valid comparisons between the mystical rites of Greece and the Orthodox sacraments.

From that which we do know, the mysteries of Greece were concerned with two deities related to the Greek Hades and the life hereafter, for, it seems, that immortality of the soul in some form was a commonly accepted belief in Greece at the time of the Eleusinian mysteries. The purpose behind that which was shown and told to the votaries by the hierophantes — the man entitled to reveal the sacred things — was to establish a friendly association between the votaries and the two deities, Demeter and Kore, and to secure a favorable reception in the world under. The object of the mysteries was, thus, to secure everlasting happiness for those who had undergone initiation and were thereby privileged with the deities who controlled the life hereafter.

In the words of Aristotle, the mystae — the initiated ones — "learned nothing, but underwent an experience and an influence," and even after their initiation they continued their membership in their own particular religious cults. There is no evidence to the effect that the mystae were, as a result of their initiation, changed inwardly to a higher degree of moral being although purity of the soul was formerly required by the hierophantes for initiation. We do not know what the hierophantes revealed by words to the votaries nor what he showed to them, but the votary of a mystery was believed to have established a mystical contact with the two deities for the purpose of ensuring favorable consideration after death. It is possible that the two lives, present and hereafter, were somehow brought into a relationship of continuity by agrarian symbols, such as corn, during the ceremony and by the enactment of a rudimentary religious drama regarding Demeter and Kore together with Pluto, the dreaded sovereign of Hades.

The fact that in the Eleusinian as well as in the Orphic mysteries a ritualistic banquet was held during which the votaries ate and drank for the purpose of symbolically effecting their mystical contact with the deities concerned, is hardly analogous to that which happens in the Orthodox Eucharist. Despite obvious similarities in terminology — due to the fact that the early Church freely used the thought and language of the Greeks — the fundamental articulation of the Orthodox Eucharist is completely foreign to the thought behind the Greek mysteries and more so to the particular understanding about man and God behind the Greek mystical rites.

In the Orthodox sacrament, the center of all things said and done is Christ who is not only the power of the life after death but the power of life in general, of material and mental manifestations not only as they appear to be but as they really are in the realm of ultimate reality. There is a difference, of course, between two agrarian deities who were primarily concerned with the fruition of material life, and so with the progress of growth in matter, and a God who, in addition to being the absolute controller of matter, is the source as well of mental life and the point of convergence of all spiritual strivings in man.

The life after death in the Christian viewing of being is not another state of life filled with sorrowful inevitableness, but the completion of life, the true state of being for which this present life is a stage of preparation. The Christian — contrary to his brother in the flesh, the pagan — does not look upon life after death as a state of personal fate that he would certainly avoid if he could; nor does he feel that he should try to make it as sufferable as possible by expiating the deities that control it.

The true Christian looks upon the life hereafter as a return to the abode of a deity which, far from being hostile to him, awaits his return as a father waits for the return of a long absent son. Even the entire kingdom of the father is reserved for the true sons of God, for those who prepare themselves in this life in such a way as to be able to understand and live the reality of the kingdom of God. The happiness, then, which the mystae sought by initiation in the mysteries is fundamentally different from the state of being in which the sons of God will find themselves in the kingdom to come. At best, the former is a state of tranquility not very much unlike living happily in this world.

While the mystae "learned nothing, but only suffered an experience and an influence," the Christian votary learns the true meaning of things by means of a new vision which he acquires as a result of his faith in Christ. The essence of things is revealed to him, and the disturbing antithesis between spirit and matter is accordingly resolved into a new reality where incongruities remain only seeming, while a new harmony between apparent and real renders human life supremely meaningful. God, man, and the world, do not stand apart from one another, as is the case in pagan cosmotheory, but are brought together into a working relationship the center of which is God; yet, everything is done for the sake of man to the extent that God takes the human form for the purpose of sanctifying the flesh and for making man the inheritor of his immaterial kingdom.

As a result of his faith in Christ and of his membership in the Church, the Christian sees life differently and acts differently among his fellow-men, but this change is not the result "of an experience and an influence" as if he were under a magic spell brought about by his initiation in the Christian mystery, for he is still in command of his willing powers and may, if he so wishes, revert to his old life. The *magic* of the Orthodox sacraments, in the essence and operation of the Grace, is conditioned by the individual's free will upon which the fruition of the Spirit in man depends. It is evident, then, that if similarities do exist between the Greek

29

mysteries and the Orthodox sacraments, these are similarities only in names, and remotely — if at all — in ceremonial procedure.

The Orthodox sacraments are fundamentally different from the Greek rites despite analogies, and stand unique not in their ceremonial procedure but in their being the highest form of religious activity for the purpose of uniting man with God, an idea that appeared in man as he was developing the understanding of his relationship to nature and God. The slight similarities between acts of pagan expiation and Christian salvation have been implicitly best explained by the Apostolic preaching and by St. Paul who developed this fundamental preaching into the first complete system of Christian theology.

The Apostles were conscious themselves of the fact that Christ Incarnate and Resurrected did not establish in the experience of man a completely new theory of life unheard of before by man. He rather fulfilled the innermost feelings and strivings of man and his purest and highest ideas concerning man and God. The uniqueness of Christianity lies in the fact that Christ did fulfill the striving of man to return to his Father through events previously unheard of in man's experience, through His Incarnation and Resurrection. Further, He established a new law in the life of man, the law of love, a kind of love with which man was totally unfamiliar before but on the strength of which the Hebrew theocratic judgment became the Christian anthropocentric love of God for man.

Another difference between the God of the Christian Eucharist and the god of the pagan theophagy is the fact, unceasingly stressed by the Apostles, that Christ lived on earth as a man among men, an historical personality experientially unlike Demeter of Eleusis or Dionysus of the Orphics, and, for that matter, even unlike the Logos of Philo and the Gnosis of the various contemporary disciplines of the East at the time. Their god appears to be little more than a figment of a religious or philosophical mind, while Christ is the Son of God who descended on earth for the sake of man. For that matter, Christ is unlike all other saviors who preceded or followed Him either as historical personalities or as figures of religious mythology. "All but one," as someone said, "whatever their claim to godhead, can make only the most dubious claims to manhood."

II

The Content and Meaning
of Orthodox Worship

Personal communication with God becomes possible only through prayer, the nature of which appears to be fundamentally supplicatory, although praying for the purpose of thanking God for that which the individual has received from above is neither infrequent nor less genuine.

In general, the depth of the personality from which prayer originates appears to equal the degree of necessity by which man is spurred to approach God in the humility of supplication. But even so, personal prayer is indicative not only of the needs and wants of the individual but of his faith in God not only as the source of good but as the Being whose relationships with man transcend the relationships of a petitioner to giver.

It is in this respect that personal prayer unavoidably includes dogmatical elements, though in a rudimentary form, and can be classified as worship. This rudimentary dogmatical background of personal prayer is not in the form of any particular theology; rather, it is based on a broad outline of Christian metaphysics by which the love of God for the ailing man has been expressed by the redemptory work of Christ and by the assurance that any man may ask for the help of God through Christ.

Such a dogmatical outline appears to be in the back of the mind of the Christian suppliant, despite the fact it is seldom expressed by the wording of his personal prayer which is usually concerned with the subject matter of his supplication. Yet, although the content of personal prayer is completely private, its constituent parts are expressive of the faith of the individual with regard to the place of man in relation to the world of phenomena and in relation to ultimate reality.

Perhaps, it is only through personal prayer that the individual finds his opportunity to live his faith before God in its most essential form despite the briefest possible terms of thought and language by which this faith is expressed. The Lord's prayer itself stands as the classical pattern of a discourse with God, based upon the wants of the individual as they appear in the context of one's faith in God's omnipotence, God's love for man, man's fragility, and man's obedience to God's will.

The Orthodox worship differs little, if at all, from the most genuine personal prayer, except that it is amplified to include the community, that is, the Church of Christ. As the individual expresses through prayer his most earnest and most inclusive faith in God and his beliefs about man and God, so does the Church express herself in terms of Orthodox worship not as a mere aggregate of believers but as a body of Christians living their faith in Christ and making thereby manifest their position with regard to the realities of life relative to God.

It is perhaps in no other form of Christian worship than in the worship of the Orthodox Church that the ritual is woven so closely with the teachings of the Church that worshipping practices become expressive of the very being and synthesis of the Church; in fact, to the extent that the Orthodox Church cannot be correctly understood and properly evaluated without a study of her ritual.

Orthodox worship is not a mere expression of the religious experience of the Orthodox in terms of ceremonial forms entered into the ritual for making it impressive or complete from the aesthetic viewpoint, but a worshipping act essentially expressive of the faith and self-awareness of the Church. Hence, the zeal with which the Church has resisted all attempts to interfere with the essentials of her worship, and the proverbial devotion of the clergy to the directory of public Worship (Typikon) by which the ceremonial treasure of the Orthodox is guarded.

As regards the essentials of its form and structure, Orthodox worship was not gradually developed by ecclesiastics and theologians for the purpose of answering the worshipping and ritualistic circumstances of the Church. Rather, these essentials are native to the very institution of the Church in the Apostolic and sub-Apostolic periods, and have always been understood to convey in terms of ceremonial acts the Biblical and Apostolic elements of Christian belief.

As such, the Orthodox worship is of authority equal to that of the teachings of the Church, inasmuch as the Church's dogmatical articulation becomes expressed in

34

terms of liturgical inter-personal experience. This explains the reason for which tradition is so much concerned with the worship of the Church, and why the Fathers so zealously adhered to it as to a decisive standard of reference while they were laboring to establish the true faith and genuine practice of Orthodoxy.

The genuineness and primitiveness of Orthodox worship can be clearly ascertained by considering the fundamental beliefs and practices on which the whole structure of the Orthodox ritual stands. As with the primitive Church and the first Christians so with Orthodox worship and with the members of the Orthodox Church, there are two fundamental presuppositions upon which a genuine Christian Church should lay her foundation: on the fact that God was revealed in the person of Christ, and on the fact that the redemption wrought by Christ is now entrusted to His Church as its guardian and dispenser.

The Meaning of the Resurrection for the Orthodox

The revelation of God through Incarnation was finally and triumphantly sealed by the Resurrection of Christ without which, "both our preaching and our faith have been in vain," in the words of St. Paul. The Cross of Christ would have remained a shameful form of Jewish capital punishment had not Christ risen from the dead. The Orthodox Church continues to stress the Resurrection of Christ with the emphasis of the very Apostolic preaching, that is, as the cardinal point of Christology upon which the whole Christian plan of redemption depends.

No other event in the life of Christ has enjoyed as high an eminence in Orthodox worship as His Resurrection to which every Sunday service in the year is primarily devoted. Sunday is not merely the Christian Sabbath devoted to God by ancient ordinance, it is the *Kyriake*, the Lord's Day, the most important day of the week because on that day Christ rose from the dead and the whole divine project of saving man by defeating the forces of this world was brought to an indisputable completion. Easter day is called by the Greeks *Lampra*, the brightest day of all, and has always been the center of the Orthodox calendar just as Christmas has been *the* day of Western Christianity.

The pre-eminence of the Resurrection in Orthodox worship is not, however, a later development, but the culminating point of the faith of the primitive Church upon which Orthodoxy based its very being as the Church of Christ entitled to perpetuate the work of salvation within the mystical body of the risen Christ, its believers. The Resurrection predominates the whole Orthodox worship not only as the central point of the ritual, but as the supreme event in the life of Christ which brings the whole teaching of the Church to its logical conclusion, the redemption of man from the world of matter.

It is precisely this aspect of worship from which the mystical trend of Eastern Christianity derives as an attempt at both personal redemption from phenomenal reality and at union with God in terms not only of the life hereafter but in terms of present-day experience as well. Without Christ's Resurrection, the Orthodox idea of deification, *theosis*, would remain an insolent philosophical bid for divinity; but with Christ's victory over death, the Orthodox mystic is enabled

to break through the barrier of matter and reach his proto-
type, the risen Christ. The Resurrection of Christ becomes
the pattern of the resurrection of man, and serves as the
starting point of a sanctifying Church commissioned to res-
urrect the believer from the state of death to which he is
subject by the very fact of his material being.

The symbolism and mysticism of Orthodox worship is in
accord with the very idea underlying the teaching and
practice of Orthodoxy by which the fundamentals of Christian revelation must not only be kept constantly alive in
the soul of the individual, but they must also be realized in
his experience as vital elements of his mental, emotional,
and moral constitution.

The Eucharist in Orthodox Worship

Apart from personal mysticism pursued on the presup-
position of Christ's victory over death, Orthodox worship
provides a more tangible situation by which the believer
can unite with Christ resurrected. This is a situation of
common worship but of individual participation in the divine
essence of Christ; the sacrament of Eucharist. Eucharist and
Resurrection constitute the core of Orthodox worship and
are considered to be the very reason for the religious activity
of the Orthodox.

On the basis of Biblical evidence and in accordance with
the practice of the primitive Church, Orthodox worship has
adhered to the Eucharist as the most important practical
aspect of the life of the Christian by which he, being finite
and fragile morally and physically, unites with God and is

actually deified if he communicates worthily of the Body and Blood of Christ.

The very Apostolic and sub-Apostolic concept of the Eucharist together with its prerequisites, faith and love, has been meticulously preserved in Orthodox worship. The position of the Orthodox Church in regard to the question of faith and love is very clearly expressed by liturgical statements and admonitions during the celebration of the sacrament of Eucharist, and constitutes, in fact, one of the most characteristic teachings of Orthodox theology.

Christ had clearly distinguished between His own love and any other kind of good relationship between man and man, and He further explicitly bequeathed to mankind the love He had for man as the model love one man should bear for another. St. Paul, repeatedly assured his correspondents that faith without love is of no avail, even if it be of the faith that moves mountains. This new concept of love is not only advocated by Orthodox worship, it is taken to be the very core of Orthodox belief and practice.

During the Liturgy and before the recitation of the Creed, the deacon calls upon the believers to love one another so that they can confess with undivided minds and hearts their faith through the words of the Creed. And when the gifts of the Eucharist, the Body and Blood of Christ, are offered for communion to the members of the Church, the deacon invites them to approach with the fear of God, with faith, and with love.

The Orthodox Liturgy — actually the celebration of the sacrament of Eucharist — is modelled after the Last Supper in the Upper Room. The liturgical Fathers of the Orthodox Church have not only preserved the original dogmatical flavor of the Orthodox ritual, but have placed the celebration of the Eucharist at the center of Orthodox worship, as the culminating point of communal relationships with man's Savior, whereby not only a divine mystery is performed but the members of the mystical body of Christ are, in terms of worship, united with one another. The celebration of the Eucharist together with the dispensation of the sacrament to the members of the Church, assure thus the everlasting continuance of the Church as the mystical body of Christ.

The constituent parts of the Liturgy also refer to important points of belief in relation to the redemptory work of Christ and in relation to the ways and means by which the individual can appropriate the divine redemption. The first part of the Liturgy consists of advancing the Word of Christ by reading from the Bible and by preaching from the pulpit. Then follow the admonitions cautioning the believers to search their hearts and minds and to see whether faith and love as the indispensable qualifications for communicating the Body and Blood of Christ are found there. Finally, the invocation of the priest for the gifts to be changed by the power of the Holy Spirit into the actual Body and Blood of Christ results in a visible continuity of the sacrifice performed on the Cross once and forever, and also affords the opportunity to the believers to be perceptibly united with Christ by faith and by means of the Holy Gifts.

The Church offers the supreme Gifts to the believers as uniting media with the Lord who, being the Head of the Church, thus unites all the members of His mystical body into one. No other worshipping act can, in terms of human experience, convey so much and effect so perfectly the sub-

39

stantiation of Christian revelation in the life of the individual.

The Orthodox Worshipping Complement and Environment

Another important aspect of Orthodox worship relates to the fact that both clergy and laity participate equally in all acts of worship. No worship can be conducted in the absence of either one of the two segments that make up the fullness of the militant Church of Christ. The clergy is the governing body, but no clergyman can perform a sacrament or, for that matter, any one of the communal acts of worship unless the laity is present.

The Eucharist can hardly be celebrated by the priest for his own benefit, because, as celebrant of the sacrament, he acts on behalf of the Whole Church and for the benefit of the entire membership of the Church. And though the clergy is the leading party in communal worship, holding any service does not depend upon their will or initiative, but rather remains the responsibility of the Church for which they act. The priest acts for both clergy and laity and only in the presence of both can the Church be considered to have been genuinely convened. The validity of the sacraments does not depend, accordingly, on the celebrant's personal qualifications and state of personality but upon the expressed will of the Church for dispensing the sacramental Grace.

The active participation of the laity in Orthodox worship is a derivative of the belief by which the complement of the Church act in their capacity as the mystical body of Christ.

Indicative of this is the fact that in the celebration of the sacraments, the Orthodox celebrant never uses the formula, "I baptize thee . . . ," or, "I marry thee . . . ," but he says, "the servant of God . . . is baptized," etc. The third person and the passive voice are invariably used in all sacraments thus showing that the one who actually performs the sacrament is not the priest but the Church through the priest.

The clergy, in the same manner as the laity, communicate of the sanctified elements at the end of the celebration of the Eucharist in their capacity as members of the Church, not as performers of the sacrament. In his inaudible prayers during the celebration of the Eucharist, the priest prays for the sanctification of the Gifts by attesting that He who offers the gifts for sanctification and He who is offered to the communicants in the form of the sanctified Gifts is Christ Himself.

The very decoration of the church is arranged in such a manner as to stress the presence in the sacraments, and above all in the Eucharist, of the whole Church, militant on earth and triumphant in heaven. The icons of the Virgin Mary and of all those who successfully fought the battle of this world and have triumphed in heaven — the saints — symbolize the fact that whenever the Orthodox Church acts as the mystical body of Christ, all of her members are present and are witnessing the union of the finite with the infinite effected for the sake of man by way of the Church acting under the guidance of the Spirit of Christ.

Orthodox hymns are composed in such a way as to advance the teaching of the Church with regard to both the redemptory work of Christ and the trust the Church received from the Lord Himself to continue this redemptory work for as along as man exists. Another favored topic of Orthodox hymnology is Christian living itself with its temptations, falls, and risings, recorded by means of ecclesiastical poetry and mystical philosophy. Greek hymnographers made a lavish use of contemplation, poetry, and philosophy —especially of Platonic thought as this developed later in Alexandria under its Hellenistic form.

As in hymnology so in ecclesiastical contemplation, the most profound thoughts and the deepest feelings relative to Greek metaphysical speculation were employed by the Fathers in their effort to clad the Christian tenets with the best garments the human mind had ever fashioned. This is because the Greek Fathers believed the products of the Greek mind to be in their essential strivings not pagan, rather forerunners of the truth which the world finally received through the revelation of Christ.

The hymns of the Orthodox Church, deeply reflective as they are of human wisdom of the highest order, are also mindful of the one gift that man cannot receive via the most profound reflection of the most profound mind; the boundless mercy of God by which alone the eyes of the soul are finally opened to a reality seen not as in a "glass darkly" but directly and unobstructively as in the days to come.

III

Teachings and Practices Characteristic of Orthodoxy

Agape in Orthodoxy

Certain teachings and practices of the Orthodox Church considered to be more or less characteristic of her faith and the way this faith has been applied in the experience of her membership will be touched upon in the following. Some of these might sound strange to ears accustomed to the legalism and stringent dogmatical conformity of Western Christianity. It should be remembered, however, that the Orthodox system of faith and order in the form of dogmatics would perhaps have never been drawn by the Fathers were it not for teachings and practices contrary to those which were implicitly accepted by the conscience of the Church everywhere. These contrary teachings and practices have been called heresies, that is, mistaken understandings and interpretations of Apostolic Christianity which, though in most cases sprang from sincere hearts, proved, nonetheless, disturbing and potentially disrupting influences within the mystical body of Christ.

The Fathers of the Church did not compose standards of faith and practice in the manner in which later theologians drew up their Confessions and theological treatises. There were no academic motives behind the statements of Faith on the part of the Fathers of the early Church; these statements were not the product of their own theological speculation but simple and precise statements of the faith of the Church, simple and precise statements of the content of the religious experience of the membership of the Church. These were convictions nested in the hearts of the believers and, as such, they constituted the credo of the membership of the Church and were practiced by everyone everywhere.

Hence derives the Orthodox teaching by which the foundation of faith is in the heart rather than in the mind. The seeds of faith are planted in the heart where they undergo the metamorphosis of growth in unison with the believer's personality and ultimately become the individual's spiritual treasure consequently expended by love (agape) in terms of personal experience. Accordingly, Confessions of Faith cannot be separated from the behavior of the Christian, and they are valid and acceptable only insofar as they express the living faith of the Church, not the speculations of people who practice dogmatics as a form of academic preoccupation or as an exercise of personal wisdom.

The Fathers of the Church were exceedingly conscious of their responsibility whenever they stated the faith of the Church in terms of theological exposition, being fully aware of the fact that they were offering propositions to be not merely mentally accepted but to be personally assumed as guides to both faith and motivating forces of behavior.

The opening words of the Creed, "I believe," have a unique significance for the Orthodox as they do not elicit a mere mental acquiescence to the statements that follow but they express the content of the believing heart of the individual, his religious convictions together with the purity of personal conscience which alone renders the mere belief a living reality. And since the animating force of the Christian is love — in the same manner in which love has been the very reason of the Incarnation of Christ — it is only logical for the believers to be called before the recitation of the Creed to love one another, for only with a loving heart and an undivided mind can the fullness of the Church confess their faith in the form of the Creed.

It is with this Pauline and Johannine concept of love that the essence of Orthodox mysticism must be identified, not with personal "mystical practices" with which it has been erroneously associated even by some members of the Orthodox Church. Mystical practices that seek to effect a union between the individual and God on a parapsychological level have never been sanctioned by the Orthodox Church as a genuine part of her experiential spectrum. Although such mystical practices have been carried on within Orthodoxy, and a number of treatises have been written by Orthodox theologians on the pattern of the writings of pseudo-Dionysius the Areopagite, the only mystical union with Christ-God of which the Church knows is the union through faith and love which, unlike its namesake of "mystical practices," is effected on the level of consciousness and in the nature of an inner transformation of man's faculties to the point where the individual lives only in Christ.

Apart from the piety of the urge to unite with Christ

that these "mystical practices" exhibit and by virtue of which alone have escaped the complete stricture of the Church, they are undoubtedly devoid of some of the most important presuppositions of Christian living, of the distinction, for example, between the inner life of sanctity and the material aspect of being. For, if one can effect by means of mental and physical exercises his union with God by effacing at will his material existence and all that it brings with it in terms of diverse strivings and conflicts, then the very concept of Christian life as a preparatory stage to ultimately being with God becomes irrelevant to the life of the Christian. The fact that these "mystical practices" presuppose purity and personal advance in the ways of God does not change their nature from "moments of ineffable experience of glory and self-realization in the boundless being of God" to a genuine Christian experience.

The truly Christian mysticism abides by the inescapable distinction of being into spirit and matter, and the union between man and Christ referred to in the Bible is called mystical in the sense that it is an inward experience as opposed to the philosophical absorption of man into the essence of God as a result of which mental and material manifestations appear to have been prematurely effaced on the initiative of the mortal man; this, contrary to the Biblical teaching by which such a state of personal being is to be experienced only in the life hereafter.

Orthodoxy as the Continuity of the Ancient Church

The Orthodox Church claims an unbroken continuity with the teachings and practices of the early Church as these were developed by Creeds — especially the Nicene and the Constantinopolitan — and by other decisions of General Councils and Synods during the first eight centuries of Christianity. This dogmatical confinement of Orthodoxy within the circumference of the seven General Councils, far from being a shortcoming, has safeguarded Orthodoxy from later dogmas of doubtful validity and authority and from forfeiting her being the only Christian Church that can lay a valid claim to the wealth of thought and practice of the undivided Church.

It is the opinion of some theologians of other Faiths that the Orthodox Church has unnecessarily prevented herself from further developing her dogmatics in the manner in which the dogmatics of the Western Church developed, especially after the Protestation of the sixteenth century. In response, we contend that if the religious truths of Christianity are in reality unconditionally true they need no further development lest man's theological genius adds elements not only foreign to the experience and thought of the early Church but incongruous, as well, with Biblical and Apostolic faith and practice. Dogmas such as those of the Trinity, Incarnation, Christology in general, man and his salvation, and eschatology — to mention only those of cardinal importance — can hardly be developed beyond the statements and interpretations of the Fathers, unless we take development to mean clarification and exposition by way of contemporary media of expression and understanding.

Following, then, on the Patristic principle by which dogmas are formulated when Orthodox teachings are put to doubt not so much from without as from within, the Orthodox Church has in practice been very reluctant to state dogmas in exact and precise logical definitions. This reluctance is not a later development but an early practice which is responsible for a number of questions left by the General Councils pending not because the Fathers did not think of developing their positions into statements of minute detail, but because the Orthodox disposition would rather avoid to present beliefs in the form of logical conclusions which, as in the case of some dogmas of other Churches, often prove to be products of mere logical play lacking the support of the conscience of the Church.

Doctrines have always been understood by the Orthodox Church to be statements of faith and practice dictated by circumstances. As such, they are preventive in nature and, consequently, void not only of the context in which they might have been entertained by the membership of the Church but of the experiential wealth, as well, and of the variety of expressions they are bound to assume as they are adopted to personal and group trends and development. At best, dogmas portray the essence of the universal faith of the Church extracted by logical conceptual abstraction but limited in scope and content. Else, a misrepresentation could ensue owing to the fact that the life of the Church, being the result of spiritual growth, is full not only of theses but of antitheses as well.

Thus, it is not difficult to understand why the Greek Fathers, being conscious as they were of the fact that Christianity is a living faith and as such depends upon the spiritual development of the membership of the Church, cared to include in their dogmatical decisions only points without which the Faith loses its identity. Believing further that Christianity is a religion of the heart rather than one of the mind, they avoided subjecting their faith in Christ to logical legalism which, as it has happened with later theologians, can put to peril the spirit of true Christianity by leading to logical conclusions outwardly valid but inwardly incongruous with the teaching and practice of the Apostolic Church which, after all, must remain the model Church for all subsequent developments in Christianity.

Accordingly, whenever a belief proves to be genuinely universal, still its statement in the form of a dogmatical teaching must wait for the full approval of the conscience of the Church finally expressed as a decision of a General Council. It is not strange, then, that though sacramental practices have become indispensable aspects of the life of the Orthodox Church, yet the teaching of the Church on the sacraments has not been formulated into dogmas.

This does not mean, on the other hand, that the Orthodox Church views later dogmatical developments in the West from a preconceived negative viewpoint. As Orthodox theology gradually goes back to the most genuinely Patristic thought, Western developments in thought and practice are approached with an unbiased and independent mind capable of rejecting non-Orthodox elements and, at the same time, of adopting developments which will strengthen the hand of the Orthodox Church in dealing with problems for which she is not exactly well equipped due to the long subjugation of most of the Orthodox countries to non-Christian invaders from the East. Western advances in the knowledge of forces and factors motivating personal and group behavior are studied by the Orthodox Church in relation to her greatest problem at the present time, the problem of the Orthodox in the society of today.

Mention must be made here of the second source of Orthodox teaching and practice, the Tradition. As it is known, the Orthodox Church derives her teachings primarily from Scripture, especially from the New Testament teaching and practice. Tradition as the second source of Orthodox thought and life is held to be as important as the evidence and witness of the New Testament itself because its contents deal with the faith and moral truths revealed by Christ and included in the books of the New Testament. This Tradition must be clearly and unmistakably distinguished from mere ecclesiastical tradition by which Church life and order are regulated and which is subject to change in response to current conditions and circumstances.

Tradition — also known as Holy Tradition — does not promulgate new teachings or new dogmas. Its contents are proven by being in full and unconditional accord with the teachings of the Bible. Tradition is not a bunch of rulings super-imposed on the life of the Church but a body of evidence on the strength of which the contents and authenticity of the very New Testament were judged by the conscience of the Church. The Canon of the New Testament —that is, the number of books that finally made up the New Testament and the standards by which they were selected — is, in fact, the product of Traditional evidence upon which the Church based her acceptance of some books and her refusal of others.

The oral tradition of the primitive Church is undeniably important seeing that written records concerning Christ and the Apostles were not only abundant but subject to constant alterations as they were copied by hand. For example, the early Creeds are part of this tradition by which genuine Biblical teachings were stated systematically for the purpose of being used as guides of faith that were later given an approved form by the General Councils.

Tradition has been often confused with ecclesiastical tradition not only by non-Orthodox but by many Orthodox as well. Considering that ecclesiastical tradition played an important part in preserving the Orthodox faith through many adversities and vicissitudes, the customary is still confused on occasion with the Traditional. As a result, customs gradually introduced by clerics for the purpose of keeping the people as close to their Church as possible have come to be recognized as Traditional. And because the customary has often proved to be stronger in the minds of some clergymen than the Traditional — due to the human fear of departing from the accepted — true Orthodox Tradition has suffered rather heavily and the Church has lost in purity of faith and order. A careful study of this situation is under way now and in time the boundaries between the customary and the Traditional will be clearly delineated lest genuine and important characteristics of Orthodoxy be terminally lost.

Orthodoxy and the Virgin Mary

The Orthodox Church has no dogma nor a body of teachings awaiting dogmatical confirmation by a General Council concerning the Mother of God. Following on the statement of the Creed by which Mary, being a Virgin, gave birth to

Christ, and in accord with early practices by which Mary was venerated by the Christians above all other servants of God, the Fathers have called her *Theotokos*, the one who gave birth to God.

This adjective by which Mary is invariably known among the Orthodox, expresses the core of the teaching of the Orthodox Church about Mary, the Mother of God. The Church has consistently adhered to this teaching through her history and has readily condemned individual practices of Mariolatry (Mary worship) in the belief that a departure from Apostolic practice, however pious in origin it may be, constitutes in itself a heresy, that is, an act of separation from the beliefs and practices of the Church.

More important, then, than isolated popular beliefs and practices concerning Mary is the fact that the Orthodox Church has remained Biblical and Apostolic in her teaching about Mary as this is made clear by the place officially ascribed to her in Orthodox worship despite a number of doubtful expressions in hymns devoted to her. The Orthodox Liturgy, being the Church's most ancient and most authoritative single document of dogmatical importance, constantly reminds the worshipper that the place of Mary in worship is honorary and has nothing to do with the worship of God, the fact that she is asked to intercede to her divine Son for the benefit of man notwithstanding.

Expressions which were furtively introduced in the Orthodox hymnal by pious monastics but which could easily be confused for worshipping acts have been substituted with the correct ones. And as the Church has come to claim her own after a period of much devotion but of little knowledge even of the writings of her own Fathers, ignorant dissidents are gradually reconfirmed in the faith of the Church by which there is only one Man who is indisputably known to have been of the divine essence as well.

However, Mary is and will forever remain for the Orthodox the Holy Mother of God, who fell asleep instead of dying, and who by necessity of human understanding and logic must enjoy in heaven a place second only to that of her Son. But the place of Mary in Orthodoxy is appreciably different from that which she has been accorded in Roman Catholic doctrine and worship. Yet, friends of the Orthodox Church have repeatedly asked the question: Why does the Orthodox Church not officially proclaim in dogmatical terms her position regarding Mary and thus dispel the impression in the minds of many that Mariolatry is an accepted practice within Orthodoxy?

Orthodoxy, following on the footsteps of the early Church, has consistently shown a marked dislike for stating religious experiences in terms of dogmatical affirmations. It rather allows its beliefs to mature, to fill the minds and hearts of its people, and thereby to create that which is known as the conscience of the Church. Whatever is alive in the conscience of the Church bears a higher degree of validity than dogmatical affirmations, seeing that no dogma can prove really valid unless it is the outcome of communal faith and practice. Doctrines which had not been formulated in the nature of statements representing the content of the conscience of the Church never proved binding irrespective of which bishop or how many bishops had been responsible for them.

The genuine content of the conscience of the Church need not be stated in terms of dogmatics unless it is seriously disputed from *within* the Church herself. Only then, the Church is convened into a Council and decides what measures should be taken to counteract the mistaken interpretation.

In the case of the place which Mary occupies in Orthodox worship, the particular type of veneration which may be confused for worship has never become part of the conscience of the Church. If certain beliefs and practices do on occasion prove insensitive to the due difference between veneration and worship, such beliefs and practices have been singled out by the Church and have been condemned as spurious and incongruous with Orthodox teaching and Tradition.

There are two reasons for which Mary enjoys such a high place of honor in the heart of the Orthodox, both connected with the particular temperament and culture of the congregations of the Orthodox Church and with the philosophy of life underlying Christianity in the East.

The first is related to Biblical information about Mary and to the esteem in which chastity and motherhood have always been held in the East. Biblical information about Mary is meager apart from two important narrations in the Gospels, the one relating to the immaculate conception of Christ and His birth, and the other relating to the presence of Mary at the drama of Golgotha. Preparatory to the whole part Mary played in the life of her Son, is the scene of Annunciation at which she is presented as the "all-gracious maiden" whom God selected to become the instrument of a unique occurrence in which the purest of all women was to be used as a vessel of ineffable Grace for the salvation of man. Unaware as Mary was at that point of the designs of God, she could not realize the nature nor the magnitude of the issues involved. Her reaction was one of bowing to the will of God by which she was to be used as the human vessel in which the Spirit was to take the physical form of man according to the laws of nature. But despite the miraculous Annunciation and the signs that followed Christ's birth, Mary retained in full her human feelings of motherhood and patiently awaited for the complete unfolding of the divine Will which, however, she never expected to include the very death of her Son.

The scene of the Annunciation and all that involved in regard to Mary's personal state of chastity and God's will about her are related in a long series of hymns which constitutes the core of weekly services during Lent, the Salutations of Mary. These hymns are particularly noteworthy for their poetry, philosophy, and their theological ideas, and are characteristic of the high esteem in which moral and bodily purity in womanhood is held with the people of the Eastern Mediterranean. Purity of the body is held to be a necessary attribute of the pure soul inasmuch as the moral realism of these people views personality behavior to be heavily conditioned by the state of the body in regard to sexual realities.

The selection of the Virgin Mary by the Spirit did not only sanctify symbolically all virgins, but also established the model maiden in society and the ideal to which every self-respecting young woman should strive. Since that time, and irrespective of racial background, Mary has stood as the ideal maiden who pleased God because of the purity of her soul as well as because of the purity of her body.

The influence of the Virgin Mary has not been limited,

however, to her being accepted as the ideal maiden; it spread further and embraced the whole state of womanhood. Since the moment Mary became the mother of Christ, she embodied in her love for Him the most tender and most dramatic feelings of motherhood as the events following the growth of her Child brought her footsteps finally before His Cross.

The love she exhibited for her Son, the fears with which His growth was associated, the wonderful signs of His true identity, and the sorrow of His being put to death, all these experiences were lived by Mary in a human way, in the very way in which a mother lives her experience of being one with her child. Thus, in the same way in which she sanctified maidenhood she also sanctified motherhood, and was taken accordingly to be the ideal mother who lives the supreme experience of her life in happiness and sorrow as every other mother does.

It is not strange, then, that Mary has always been, at least in the East, the Holy Virgin and the Holy Mother. Who can better understand the turmoil of womanhood in its most important states of being — virginity and motherhood — than Mary herself who played a role in man's history that no other woman has ever even dreamed for herself? Is it possible that Mary could refuse to somehow help a virgin in distress and a mother in sorrow?

It is the position of Mary as the ideal of womanhood, and by logical necessity as the patron of helpless maidens and suffering mothers, that is responsible for individual practices of Mariolatry; even though in cases such as these the person of Mary has never been confused with the person of Christ nor the respective place each holds in the scale of eternal values has ever been in doubt.

The second reason for which the position of Mary has been so high in the esteem and worship of the Orthodox is the belief of the Church to the effect that man's redemption could not have been complete had not womanhood been involved in it. However passive the role of Mary may have been in the divine drama, hers has been the role of linking and binding together the strivings of men and women since the beginning of time to return to the heavenly abode from which they exiled themselves.

Feelings differ appreciably between man and woman and, what is most important, their attitudes toward life, including behavior mechanics by which each expresses his own particular way of being and becoming, are not exactly the same with the two sexes. This duality of feeling, willing, and living — the outcome in the opinion of some theologians of the original sin — tends to create division in mankind and often results in profound antitheses between the two sexes the bridging of which has been the object of serious efforts in the field of personal relationships. And though the soul is believed to be the same in both man and woman, yet its experiential manifestations by way of one's personal living is certainly different in man and woman.

Christ did not only offer redemption to both men and women but found the opportunity to deal in particular with womanhood in some of its most striking phases involving pain and moral failure. The fact that Christ was born in this world by a woman, instead of suddenly appearing in some place as He could, proves not only His humanity in full but the fact that by His Incarnation man and woman were united spiritually by an act of God involving the union of the finite with the infinite through the womanhood of Mary.

Mary is thus considered to be the only woman by whom the union and unity of manhood and womanhood was effected, and so the only woman through whom the equality between the two sexes was divinely established contrary to both Hebrew and pagan concepts of womanhood. The concept of woman being a mere child-bearing machine was thus destroyed forever in the minds of men, and women were readily accepted by the Christians to be the instruments of God just as men themselves were believed to be. It is Mary who freed the woman from her believed sole mission of reproduction and together with her role as mother made her the true helpmate of man and his indispensable complement.

Such a woman as Mary, the Orthodox believe, who was sanctified by having nurtured in her God Himself and who loved Him in the most pure and most human terms of motherly devotion, cannot but hold a distinguished place in the kingdom of her Son, and cannot but be sympathetic with the struggles of men and women to free themselves from the pain and suffering of material strife.

Accordingly, the Orthodox believes that if Christianity is to prove effective not only in terms of man's mind but in terms of man's emotions and strivings as well, the Mother of God must be given a place in the Christian cosmotheory second only to that of her Son. In fact, she must be the *Panagia* of the Greeks, the holiest and the greatest servant among the servants of God.

Image Worship or Icon Veneration?

An objective discussion of the place of icons in Orthodox worship is a rather difficult undertaking owing to certain abuses within the Orthodox Church and to ignorant accusations from outside the Church. Many Orthodox theologians have on occasion been caught between the image worship on the part of certain Orthodox and the iconoclasm of seemingly liberal thinkers. Between the two opposing views lies, often unnoticed, the genuine Traditional stand of the Orthodox Church by which neither the miraculous powers of icons as material objects are confirmed nor the belief that the sacred icons of the Orthodox are rejectable on the supposition that they lead to idolatry.

The arguments on both sides are extremely important for Christians in general because they involve fundamental issues relating to the content and development of the religious sentiment of the individual. It is on the strength of the issues to be outlined in the following that icons in Orthodox worship should be discussed; not on the basis of practices by which varying views are stretched to their breaking points on both sides.

Idolatry constitutes a regress to primitive religious magic and is unacceptable on the premise of the very definition of Christianity as the religion of powers permeating matter but not originating from it. The concept of the idolatric miracle is bound to stay irrational since it presupposes no intelligent power behind and beyond the miraculous manifestation, thus limiting the supernatural within the natural and bringing its whole argument to an untenable conclusion. How can a material object cause occurrences that at once evade and overrule the laws of matter to which the object itself owes its very being in time and in space? Inasmuch as the powers of the idol cannot be accounted for as originating from an intelligence superior to the one by which matter is governed, the idolatric miracle will by necessity remain hidden and unaccountable.

On the other hand, the Christian miracle is clearly ascribed to an intelligence superior to the intelligence controlling material being, but not outside the understanding of man, since the very fundamentals of Christian cosmo-theory are based not only on the existence of such superior intelligence but also on its ability to make itself manifest by means of matter and for the sake of man. As such, the Christian miracle is not a hidden and unaccountable occurrence in the experience of man. It cannot happen except on the basis of a certain design involving the Will of God and the understanding of man. Christ exercised His miraculous powers for certain reasons that all were within His Father's designs for man, not merely in response to man's asking for a miracle.

Another fundamental difference between the Christian miracle and the powers idols were believed to possess is the fact that since there is no intelligence behind the idol, miracles should either happen for the asking on the part of man or not at all. How could a piece of matter effect a miracle when it could not possibly judge the circumstances under which man was asking for it? Even if we suppose that the worship of an idol was really intended for the pagan god it represented, this god was considered to be little more than a man with magic powers which he used not because of the love he had for man but because of his personal dealings with particular individuals.

The God of the Christians does not work miracles simply on demand. On the other hand, He often does work miracles in the life of man for which man has never asked. The Christian miracle is not an interference in the course of matter for the sake of proving the powers of God over nature and man, but a divinely calculated event to help the faithful soul find the course of action which will bring it closer to God. So, the Christian miracle is not a sign and a proof of the being and powers of God but rather the hand of God extended to man for his salvation. The asking of the individual often proves irrelevant to the Will of God, and this is the reason for which few observable miracles have really occurred in the experience of man.

Obviously, miraculous Christianity stands distinctly apart from idolatric magic, and any practices that tend to lower Christianity to the level of idolatry are rightly considered to be rejectable. It is apparent, also, that those who accuse the Orthodox of image worship have in mind the type of worship just outlined. But does the Orthodox really look upon his icons in the manner in which the pagan worshipped his idol? Every thoughtful Orthodox is in a position to show, beyond doubt, not only that the normal practice of icon veneration has nothing to do with idol worship, but even cases of icon worship on the part of the more naive from among the members of the Orthodox Church is far from being unmistakably idolatric.

Before proceeding to outline the genuine Orthodox practice, the psychological soundness and theological legitimacy of icon veneration should be briefly discussed as a practice deriving from a fundamental principle in religious life without which all religions, including Christianity, degenerate into mental exercises and philosophical meditation.

Christianity is basically and primarily the religion of the individual, a series of historical events together with faith in that which these events meant to convey to man by way of his perceptive and conceptual apparatus. The redemption offered by Christ did not, in the least, invalidate man's mental or emotional faculties, nor did it change them into an extrasensory apparatus for the purpose of understanding or living the teachings of Christ. The Incarnation proved beyond doubt that God willed man not only to retain his mental, willing, and emotional powers, but to use them as channels through which alone could redemption finally pass into his waking experience.

Had man's perceptional powers been altered to a degree incongruous with the nature of present-day life, living in this world for the purpose of preparing one's soul to inherit the kingdom of God would be meaningless. The Incarnation itself would have been rendered superfluous had the teaching of Christ been designed for a man devoid of faculties capable of dealing with phenomenal reality. The miracles, the Cross, and the Resurrection of Christ, were events in time and within the world of matter. Christ was a real person to His disciples, one whom they had to know by means of their perceptual equipment and one whose strangeness consisted in His having a perfectly normal personality but in a fullness and on a level unknown to them before.

Even after the Holy Spirit empowered them to go out and preach about this unique Man, the Apostles did not betray any signs of change as far as their mental, emotional, and willing faculties were concerned. On the contrary, they employed every faculty at their command in their effort to fully appropriate the spirituality of their Master's message, and, in fact, their success depended upon such fundamental processes as cognition, thinking, willing, and feeling. The faith in Christ they preached was expected to permeate man's whole personality, and the change they sought thereby to effect in the individual was a higher state of being but within the spectrum of ordinary waking life. It seems, then, that we have still to climb from the perceptual and material to unconditional knowing and to pure being; then and only then man's instruments of contacting phenomenal reality are believed to be finally superseded.

As long as Christ was with His disciples, the experience of personal contact with Him satisfied their desire to be with the Master, but after His ascension the Apostles were left with only His memory image and with that which He said and did. Naturally, they wanted to keep their emotional and spiritual contact with Him alive, and used to gather together for the purpose of being with the Master in the spirit. In gatherings of this nature, the Apostles employed certain media of contact such as the Last Supper He held with them in the Upper Room together with hymns relating to His person and to the happenings of His life with them.

Later on, when the membership of the Church could have no first hand information about Christ, the Apostolic narrations relating to that which He said and did proved to be a very dear and a very sacred heritage. Apostolic sayings about Him, His very name and the symbols or words designed to signify Him, gradually became very important as media by which the Lord was not only portrayed to be with them but was actually believed to be with them, though only in a spiritual way. This type of spiritual and emotional contact with the Lord proved later to be the only means by which a persecuted Christian could voice his faith in Christ and at the same time could effect a kind of union with Him.

It is understandable, then, why these media of perpetuation of the memory of Christ among His followers assumed an emotional significance reaching the very depths of the personalities of the disciples of the new religion. Furthermore, the tragic developments in which the Christian Church found herself almost since the time of her inception, made signs, symbols, and expressions relating to Christ not only perceptional media by which the Lord was kept alive in the hearts of Christians but symbols as well of personal martyrdom for the name of the Lord.

Hence the sacred character which all those means of contact with the Lord assumed very early in the life of the Church and the reverence with which they were treated by the Christians to whom they had become by now not only tokens of the Master's presence among them but tokens of their identification with Him by way of following upon His very martyrdom. This must be the meaning of the inscriptions and drawings found in catacombs, and the signs of recognition which one Christian gave to another in an atmosphere in which the militant Church of Christ had already begun to triumph in heaven.

Later on, portraits of Christ aiming at a representation of His human form were designed for the same purpose as that of the symbols of primitive Christianity, that is, for the purpose not only of portraying the human countenance of the Lord but for symbolizing, as well, His divine nature.

This may have been the reason for which early iconography has little to do with art except insofar as as the human form drawn can be recognized as belonging to Christ or to other persons connected with Christ. Even much later, when iconography developed into an art properly, the same attitude toward the object of painting was exhibited by the artist who appears to be interested in showing the inner light on the face of the painted Christ or saint rather than in conforming with a realistic picturing of the outward appearance of the body.

The iconography of the Orthodox Church has remained to this day in the nature of depicting the intangibility of the soul rather than the form of the body. It has never been appreciably influenced by the Renaissance with its care to present the body in its dimensional depth and realism. The technique of the Byzantine painters became, thus, standardized in regard to depth and realism — to which as a matter of course little attention was paid — and differs from artist to artist only in the synthesis of the subject matter. The selection of the subject matter itself is more often than not of an eschatological nature, and whenever historical events are depicted they are presented in such a way as to hint to their metaphysical significance, if at all possible.

Portraiture of the members of the triumphant Church of Christ differs little from person to person in regard to individual features, but great care is taken by the artist to present in terms of facial expression the depth of the personality and the quality of the soul of the depicted saint. Contrary to Western religious painting in which the physical appears to be stressed as though the artist subconsciously attempts to present the triumphant Church by means of figures of the members of the militant Church, the Orthodox artist has always presented the triumphant Church by means of bodies the austerity and outworldliness of which not only inspire awe but create at times the sense of being in the midst of an ethereal world.

It is not strange, then, that the Orthodox tends to see in the icon of a saint not a beloved person in the way in which one person looks at the photograph of another, but the soul of the depicted person in its struggle to redeem itself from this world. Saints are often called athletes of faith, a name which every Christian believes to apply at one time or another to himself as he wrestles the forces of evil. And since the icons of the Orthodox stress the struggle and strife more than the serenity of peace and victory, the individual— being engaged as he is in constant struggle to defeat his spiritual adversaries — feels an identity with a saint depicted in a Byzantine icon which probably no Christian in the West could experience by viewing a Renaissance painting.

It appears, thus, that the affinity between a portrayed hero of faith on an Orthodox icon and the individual member of the Church cements a psychological bond between the icon and the worshipper that often proves to be as effective as if the pictured saint were in fact present in the *iconostasion* — the room corner where the family prays. This relationship between the believer and his icon entails, accordingly, a system of feelings on the part of the individual such as reverence, admiration, awe, and a conviction of patronage which the depicted saint must extend to the individual concerned. In thus reaching the person depicted on an icon, the Orthodox lives some intricate phases of his religious sentiment, mystical in nature insofar as they follow upon the Platonic pattern of reaching the Ideas of ultimate reality by means of their reflections through experiential forms.

One barely needs to mention at this point the common practice of venerating secular symbols, monuments, flags, and other objects that exert a deep psychological influence upon people who know their significance and subscribe to the ideas behind them. Countless young men have offered their lives for their flags, obviously not for a striped piece of colored cloth but for that which that piece of cloth symbolized to them, in the same manner in which countless Christians died for the sign of the Cross.

This is not to deny, however, that a number of Orthodox have on occasion resorted to indefensible practices. Some people, being ignorant of the true significance of the icons in Orthodox worship, have resorted to a crude materialistic mysticism by which the belief in the miraculous powers of God has been confused with certain icons believed to possess a miraculous power of their own. Characteristic, though, of such beliefs and practices — whenever they occur — is the fact that most of the icons considered to be miraculous depict the Mother of God, and their worshippers are, for the most part, members of the female sex.

It is not difficult for an uneducated woman to misunderstand the belief of the Orthodox Church that Mary is really the first among the triumphant servants of God and to enter, because of personal situations, the state of worship of another woman who has played such a great part in man's miraculous salvation by Christ. But characteristic also of the most simple and the most crude beliefs in the miraculous icons of Mary is the fact that these women never speak of the icons as performing the miracles, but of *Her Grace* being instrumental in the miraculous happening.

The Church has condemned the belief that an icon, as such, is capable of performing a miracle and is consequently worthy of the worship that belongs to God. At the same time, the Seventh Council at Nicaea condemned the iconoclasts as being irreverent and unmindful of an ancient practice of the Church by which icons were venerated, but the honor and reverence ascribed to them was intended for the person depicted on them.

Miraculous happenings, especially cures, connected by the faith of the people concerned with certain icons have been attested in the past and are still attested by means of objective medical and juridical investigation. But here again, it is not the icon that performs the miracle but the Grace of God which, as with the Incarnation, can act in the experience of man through matter which, in the Orthodox cosmotheory, is not intrinsically evil and therefore rejectable as a channel through which God can manifest His Will about man. It is not, then, the icon which is responsible for the miracle but the faith of the individual channeled through a material object of sacred meaning and significance, the faith that can move mountains and which, in this case, views the icon as an experiential link between human and divine.

This kind of association between the individual and the divine by means of tangible reality appears to be a necessity which will remain with the religious sentiment of the individual probably forever. Reaching God through purely immaterial means is rather an ideal state which the average individual has yet to attain. In terms of psychological situations, even image worship appears to be understandable —

though rejectable on a Christian basis as it refers to and derives from a realistic conception of religion that is usually entertained by the average individual.

Theologically speaking, miracles connected with saints, their relics or their icons, are undoubtedly not the work of the saints or their relics and icons. God, however, can render the saints together with their relics and icons instruments so to say, of His divine operation in the experience of man for the purpose of the individual's salvation.

The icons and the frescos of the Orthodox Church, in addition to being the means by which a religious sense of identity between believers and depicted saints is effected, also signify in vivid experiential terms the essence and fullness of the Church as consisting of both living and departed saints who are thus symbolically united with one another. In this respect, the bowing and kneeling before the icons and their being kissed by the Orthodox congregation can hardly be taken to constitute idolatry. The Greeks do not speak of kissing their icons but of *aspasmos*, a term devoid of its English corporeal connotation and meaning obeyance, loyalty, devotion. The Greeks do not use the same terms for kissing an icon and for kissing a person whether in a friendly or in an erotic manner.

Characteristic also of the true meaning of icon veneration with the Orthodox is the fact that before kissing an icon one always makes the sign of the cross as if to show that the veneration advanced by him to the depicted saint is in the name of Christ. As the ancient Christians embraced one another after giving the sign of recognition — the sign of the Cross — so the Orthodox people repeat this ancient act as an important token of the unity that exists between all members of the mystical body of Christ, living and dead.

The Orthodox Concept of Eschatology

Significant of the stress which the Orthodox Church lays upon this life as the necessary preparatory stage of winning the kingdom of God, is the limitation of her concept of eschatology within the teaching of the New Testament and particularly within that which Christ taught in regard to things to come.

New Testament passages dealing in a prophetic manner with the state of life hereafter are rather neglected in preference to passages dealing with this life as the all-important step toward life everlasting. Sayings of Christ such as the Sermon on the Mount, the Lord's prayer itself, the parables of ultimate judgment, and other situations pertaining to the way of life congruous with the kingdom of God, are particularly emphasized in an attempt to show that whatever the mode of the last judgment may be by God's Will and whatever the states of eternal life and eternal damnation may consist of, it is this life that will make the difference between heaven and hell for all of us. The fundamental Orthodox eschatological belief consists, then, of the very message of the whole New Testament by which the way of life of each will determine his justification or condemnation in the second coming of the Lord.

Therefore, there is no particular dogma on things to come characteristic of the Orthodox Church over and above the teachings in the Creed and in the New Testament. The

Fathers preferred to leave the state of life hereafter to the inconceivable and unknowable Will of God. Consequently, the Orthodox Church rejects ideas, such as the purgatory, which tend to suggest interference on the part of the visible Church in the synthesis of the invisible and triumphant assembly of the true servants of God.

The Orthodox Church stresses, above all, the fatherhood of God and the brotherhood of men together with the explicit statement of Christ to the effect that those who live by the laws of faith and love will be rewarded by the mercy of God with a life devoid, "of pain, sorrow, and sighs," in the words of the hymnographer. Future judgment is, thus, the final justification of the true sons of God and the perpetual condemnation of those who lived without faith and love and so in contempt of the Holy Spirit.

The memorial services for the Church's departed members conducted as acts of common prayer are really acts of supplication of the divine mercy for the benefit of the faithfully departed on the ancient practice of praying for both living and dead. But neither the degree to which the prayers of the Church prove to the benefit of her departed members nor the manner in which these may benefit them have been stated by the Church. Isolated opinions of certain Fathers and of later theologians pertaining to this question have never been sanctioned by the conscience of the Church so as to constitute official standpoints.

Just as we do not know whether our prayers are going to be answered even in matters pertaining to this life, so we cannot know whether, or in which cases, our prayers benefit our departed brothers. The Orthodox Church believes that it is not for man to know the Will of God and the manner in which it operates. The Orthodox memorial services strengthen the unity of the Church on earth and in heaven, and keep the continuity of life unbroken by extending the law of love even beyond the grave.

The emphasis which the Orthodox Church places upon this life is not only in agreement with the New Testament teaching but reasserts Christ once more as the only hope of man who, now more than ever, needs Christ to live advantageously his advanced technological way of life and to turn to his benefit rather than to his destruction the harnessing of the laws of matter he has achieved. The more man achieves his emancipation from the laws of matter the more he needs a spiritual content for his life lest a monstrous control over nature lead him back to the sin of pride and self-deification for which Christ shed His Blood so that man be redeemed from his own self.

Mysticism in General

The aim of mysticism is sublime; to unite the individual with the divine. And considering the fact that as a religious practice mysticism is not limited to Christianity, one has to interpret mystical practices as a bold thrust on the part of man to tear the blind of finite experience and enter a state of personal self-fulfillment that words cannot describe but the votive can experience.

As such, mysticism embodies the human yearning for a higher sphere of existence, a yearning that all of us clearly feel at times as a mute but unmistakable force at the foundation of our very existence. And irrespective of the

72

achievements of mystical practices — since these can never be objectively verified — the mystical tendencies that all of us carry in our souls in one degree or another play an important part in rendering our experience purposeful in our own eyes and in finally orienting it toward the eternal rather than the temporal.

The average intelligent individual is a mystic of one sort or another, even if he never suspects it. This, because man's spirit is in itself and by itself free from material bondage and can thrust upward unhindered in an attempt to fulfill itself. Often, however, this upward thrusting ends up in a tragedy for us because the spirit has to drag with it the heart — the emotional and willing faculties of the human self — a labor that most of the times proves beyond its powers.

All kinds of attempts to escape reality and enter a world devoid of conflict, from the world of the narcotic to the fantasy world of the insane, are basically mystical, although not religiously so. The difference between true religious mysticism and the outworldliness of a chemically extended personality lies in the fact that religious mysticism does not leave behind the normal experience of the individual but it tries to elevate it to the height of the ascending spirit and thus allows the whole self to enter an experience of a higher order. The chemically induced personality extension of the drug addict suppresses the waking experience of the individual to the point of complete obliteration. Hence, the return to normalcy is extremely painful.

The objective, then, of religious mysticism is to bring the sane individual to a state of being as close to that of deity as possible. This means that the waking experience of the

Christian mystic must be under constant and progressively higher development, else his attempts at reaching a higher state of being will degenerate to the escape objectives of the drug addict. This means also that a Christian mystic must be a Christian of the highest order in terms of Christian living, else he is not much different from the drug addict.

A chemically extended personality aims at no particular objective apart from that of escaping its own waking experience. There is no ideal point for identification nor a personal will to direct the self toward it. It merely jumps into a state of half-existence, the nature of which is determined by the properties of the chemical substances taken and by the way they affect the brain. The addict does not seek a higher state of being but merely a state of oblivion, a complete erasing of his waking experience and its replacement with an experience void of conflicts. The resulting experience is fundamentally pleasurable primarily because of its being devoid of conflicting personal situations and, as such, it is indeed a third dimension. But since this temporary personal elation is unreal inasmuch as it does not include the waking faculties of the individual, the addict's personality becomes progressively untidy and his waking life more and more miserable.

On the other hand, a kind of a religious mysticism is practiced even today in the nature of a series of mental and physical exercises that aim at inducing a sense of outworldliness irrespective of the fiber of one's personality and irrespective of his viewing of himself in the midst of the cosmos and in relation to the person of God. And though mystics of this kind speak of religion, the definite and well-defined relation between man and God that renders religion alive and worth-living is lacking.

We claim Christian mysticism to be fundamentally different from practices of this kind. A clarification, then, is in order, so much so that the labeling of the Orthodox Church by some as a *Church of mystics* — rather in a derogatory sense — is due to a great extent to people and practices from within the Orthodox ranks.

The Nature of Orthodox Mysticism

The only kind of mysticism which would be in line with the claim of the Orthodox Church to be fully Apostolic is the mysticism of St. Paul which, though expounded by way of terms borrowed from Neoplatonism, has nothing to do with ideas and practices promulgated by the writings of pseudo-Dionysius the Areopagite and others.

St. Paul's mysticism is in harmony with his primary concept of union with Christ through faith and love. But this union is mystical only in the sense that it is effected in an inward experience of oneness with divinity which, however, does take place on the level of consciousness — the latter being understood in its psychological connotation.

The union between individual and Christ is a conscious state, however indescribable it may be, and has nothing of the *ecstasis* by which later Christian mysticism, in both East and West, has been denominated. Furthermore, the Pauline union with Christ is a stable and lasting state of inner sanctification which differs basically from those moments of *ineffable experience* which are characteristic of

Neoplatonism and of the form by which this was expressed by pseudo-Dionysius, St. Maximus, Erigena, and others.

St. Paul's mysticism is a psychological situation which can be studied, however imperfectly, by way of the sufferer's introspection, and, above all, in the behavior in which it did issue. The other mystical experiences are parapsychological in nature and, as such, cannot withstand an objective study inasmuch as the faculty through which the mystical union is allegedly effected is no part of our media of cognition.

The conversion and subsequent mystical experiences of St. Paul are certainly not of the nature of parapsychological phenomena mainly because during those occurrences the subject was conscious of his being, of his identity, and, above all, of his moral status. The content of Pauline mystical experiences refers to situations of life with which consciousness is associated, and that which takes place is not an indescribable merging of the human with the divine but an inward identification between the ways of life of the individual and the ways of God.

The fact that mystical experiences were practiced by Orthodox ascetics and other mystics does not make them any more characteristic of Orthodoxy than similar practices in the West are characteristic of the Roman Church. The Orthodox Church has been all along fully aware of mysticism as a private practice among certain Orthodox, but she never sanctioned it as a constituent part of her spiritual and moral articulation. The Orthodox Church has officially condoned no mysticism other than that of St. Paul, save the kind of symbolic mysticism that issues from her ritual. The Orthodox idea of deification must, accordingly, be interpreted to refer to the Pauline mystical union with Christ through faith and love.

It is obviously for this reason that Orthodoxy stresses the concept of Christian love so much, for without love no inward oneness with Christ is possible. Any other interpretation of Orthodox mysticism is bound to prove philosophical rather than Christian because of the negation — inherent with all kinds of mysticism other than that of St. Paul — of the divinely revealed truth and of the concept of man needing the hand of God to be redeemed. The context, then, in which Orthodox mysticism should be understood is that of a stable state of personality in which God and man become identified because of oneness of will, on the pattern of the union of the infinite with the finite effected in the Incarnation of Christ.

Besides, the value of Orthodox mysticism does not derive from the experiences of the mystics, but it is to be found in its underlying urge of the human soul to escape its material confines and fulfill itself in another world befitting its inherent purity and non-material nature. It is this inward urge upward that the Orthodox Church expresses by her Liturgy, the most mystical and yet most pragmatic single document and single communal act of worship.

St. Paul's mystical union with Christ through faith and love and the Church's liturgical union of the individual with Christ form the only true mental, emotional, and real foundation of Orthodox mysticism by which the latter can be unmistakably distinguished from current and future artificially induced extensions of the human personality. Any other interpretation of Orthodox mysticism leads to credu-

77

lity and is bound in the long run to prove libelous to the Orthodox Church, however pious its intent may be.

Christian Unity and the Orthodox Church

As the Christian Churches are now engaged in appraising in depth and extent the resultant new dimensions of personal and group living from the thunderous social, cultural, and spiritual changes of the last few years, and as they are in the process of rediscovering and realigning their spiritual forces for the purpose of totally serving man amidst men and under God, the little flame of unity that was lighted only a few years ago has not gone out but has spread quietly and underneath the burning fires of our present crises and has kept the Christian heart warm and hopeful.

And though we have not witnessed during the last two years any new spectacular movements in institutional breaking down of dogmatical barriers, our encounters on the inter-Church level have been really and truly productive even as unheralded as they might have been. But above these formal encounters of minds and hearts on the theological level, an air of brotherhood has definitely breezed its divine warmth into the hearts of all genuine Christians and is strengthening their belief that the time when people will recognize one another solely on their bond in Christ is nearer now than ever before.

The Orthodox Church has invested in the movement for Christian Unity a considerable amount of her spiritual resources to the point of risking, on occasion, her own inner peace and ecclesiastical order. Therefore, the Orthodox viewpoint on this matter should be correctly understood seeing that many from within and without the Orthodox Church have difficulties in properly evaluating the Orthodox stand as this has been, by word and deed, expounded by the Ecumenical Patriarch Athenagoras I.

What has developed by now into the official ecumenical associations on both the national and international levels was called for as early as 1921 by the Ecumenical Patriarchate. And as soon as the World Council of Churches began functioning as a world body, the Ecumenical Patriarchate did not hesitate to be represented in it and asked the rest of the Orthodox Churches to do likewise. In 1967, the Ecumenical Patriarch Athenagoras took a historic initiative for the purpose of advancing Christian unity between Orthodox and Roman Catholics being in division for almost one thousand years.

As a result of the repeated meetings and consultations between the Patriarch and Pope Paul VI, East and West can face each other without guilt and can turn heavenward and in humility thank our Father for not having allowed us to continue hating each other anymore. An inner sense of brotherhood has been established — for being sons of the same God and brothers in the same Christ. Our institutional pride has been dulled, our eyes have been sharpened to seek out similarities and the best in each other, not the points of division and the vulture of hatred that feeds on personal and group pride, on delusions of uniqueness and suppressive supremacy, on tribal fanaticism and theological warmongering. We are in a state of humane religious treatment of each other; we even exhibit a considerably high level of theological tolerance of each other; we are, indeed, in the process of being reborn within the One Universal Church of Christ.

But we are not sacramentally united. We still adhere each to his own dogmatical viewing of the Church, and we still function and grow in Christ each within his own cultural and historical environment. But if we continue the ecumenical movement it will lead us to a oneness on principles that will ultimately rule our thinking and our actions.

And yet *the common sacramental chalice* of which Patriarch Athenagoras spoke and speaks, is in a figurative and yet very real sense being shared already by East and West. When our heads bow together in prayer, and when our hearts lie heavy even by the mere reminder of a whole millenium of division, the Biblical remorse rings loud and tearing, "Where shall I hide from my sins and Thy anger?" And our wordly glory and power are crushed to nothing. Then, as we find ourselves together in the anguish of the nightmare of divided Christ, we together drink damnation for the past but purification and hope for the future. Every priest and every congregation who have felt this way and have gone through states of inner being such as these, have drunk from the common cup of the Crucified and Risen Christ. It is this common cup that the Patriarch offers to all those, Orthodox and non-Orthodox, who are in a position to discern between the human and the divine, between the eternal and the temporal.

A derivative of this concept of the *common cup* is what has been called the theology of reconciliation that was first introduced by the Ecumenical Patriarch. It should be understood that this kind of theology is not a theology of appeasement, that is, a dogmatical retreat for the purpose of finding favor with stronger Churches and thus having adverse circumstances at home softened up. Actually, it is not a theology as such, but an attitude required of all those who now and in the future are to hew out and sculpture the monolith of Christian reconciliation.

Contrary to what has happened for a thousand years, the dialogue between East and West should be conducted not on differences but on points of common beliefs and practices. Only on the strength of common beliefs and brotherly spirit could the differences be properly viewed, honestly understood, and forgivingly settled. Up to now, the divided Christian Churches were thriving on differences between themselves as if these constituted their true characteristics and their strength as Churches of Christ.

Indeed, all of us have been guilty of viewing at times our own particular Church solely on the strength of her points of dispute with the others, not on the strength of her own positive synthesis and contribution toward the common goal of bringing Christ to the hearts of people. Much of our modern Christian theology is, explicitly or implicitly, a theology of embroilment, an attempt at gaining stature and prestige by proving one another wrong on important points of belief and practice. But the eminence that can be pieced together from the spoils and litter of a battleground is not the eminence that Christ requires of us either as individuals or groups. Our theology of reconciliation is exactly the opposite of the theology of embroilment to which we were used till now.

Obviously, the importance of Christian unity for the Orthodox Church in America is immense. Her membership is part and parcel of the American society and as such they are exposed to the current social and cultural turmoil, as well as to changing policies and national fortunes. In matters which invite and invoke a religious and moral attitude, the people look to their Church for guidance. It would be a grievous mistake on the part of the Orthodox Church to refuse — in response to the current spirit for a new relationship between peoples of diverse and often contrary attitudes and stations in society — to share the demand for unity on the excuse that she cannot mix with "heretics and schismatics." This would attest, on our part, to sectarianism, fanaticism, institutional pride and, above all, lack of Christian charity.

If the Orthodox Church is to survive in this country and finally to assume her proper place in the hearts of her own people, let alone in society at large, she will not survive as a religious ghetto, and as a kind of privileged by definition religious community. We expect our Church to survive but in the open and only after a struggle to substantiate her claim of being truly Orthodox, that is, of correctly believing and correctly practicing. This, not by keeping the Orthodox people in spiritual and ecclesiastical seclusion from fear of becoming polluted, but by allowing us to offer our minds and our hearts, our wisdom and our theology, our ritual and our religious arts and crafts and, above all, our Orthodox purity; our traditional purity which has nothing to do with the pride generating from the notion of being the greatest but is more akin to the humility generating from the notion of being the least in the service of Christ.

The movement of Christian unity does not aim at steamrolling dogmatical landmarks and at creating a unified Christian Church with a mechanical heart and a computerized brain. What it does aim at is to give back to the universal Church of Christ the heart she lost to institutional wealth, glory, and pride, together with the ability to generate anew the measure of love needed for reasoning out correctly the Fatherhood of God and the brotherhood of men. As such, it is the most blessed event that has issued from the weary heart of civilized mankind in the twentieth century, a saving counterbalance to our ability to instantly destroy each other.

IV

Facing the Present and the Future

Viewing the Miraculous

St. Luke has sketched for us in his Gospel the Annucia-
tion story by way of a few paragraphs the classical simplicity of which has survived in Byzantine iconography and
is impressively exhibited in a situation in which the idyllic
set-up of human emotionality freely and effectively inter-
mingles with its divine message.

The messenger of God visits Mary the Virgin and an-
nounces to her that she, from among all women, has been
favored by God to give birth to His only begotten Son
ordained to offer divine love and salvation to the soul of
man, a soul as perplexed as ever in the midst of an equally
perplexed group experience.

To the astonished wondering of Mary regarding the
biological *how* since she knew no man, the angel replies with
an answer that most of us have difficulty in understanding
even today. The Spirit of God, he said, will descend on
you and the fruit of his visit will be called holy, that is,
outworldly in the midst of the world.

From the Orthodox viewpoint, the Annunciation is the foundation stone of the whole Christian system of belief and practice. No chiseling whatsoever can be allowed lest we destructively touch upon the very nature and divine integrity of the Christian Gospel. Yet the story needs to be rendered understandable and acceptable in the light of that which the mind of man has penetrated up to now. Only then, it will appear credible, that is, relevant to present-day modes of thinking and living.

Most of today's adults have been reared within the atmosphere of the miraculous in Christianity and either do not feel the need for or do not dare to question even for a moment Biblical narratives of this kind. Perhaps, it is for this reason that the personal Christianity of most of us proves in case of need so disappointingly inadequate of supporting us on an acceptable level of inward sanity.

However, present-day personal and group spiritual fragility requires that we unavoidably face squarely and courageously the whole issue of our religion in relevance to both how we view life and the world today and how we reach our conclusions regarding some such capital problems as that of man against the assumption of God's being and God's presence in our midst. This is actually the problem of rendering Christianity relevant not merely to our cultural patterns of thinking and living but to our searching for an inner anchor in the material and spiritual vastness of creation.

In pursuing, though, this kind of end, we will have to touch not only upon semantics and symbols but upon the very foundation of Christian belief. This, for the purpose of cementing an unbreakable adhesion between dogma and that which man's mind and heart have been tutored into as a result of unprecedented advances in recognizing our environment in a cosmic dimension and in the face of the limitless boundaries of human thought in its bid for self-discovery.

That which follows is not intended to rationally solve the ever-present question of the miraculous in Christianity. Rather, to merely point out to religiously alert individuals the very old and very new Patristic line of thought regarding a problem that cannot any more be summarily dismissed on the ground that there can be no scientific evidence for it.

True, the Annunciation story can easily be dismissed as a myth if measured by the yardstick of logical argumentation and inevitableness on the strength of the fact that we have no historical evidence for it. That is what materialists have done all along the history of Christianity, and that is what some of us do even today although without openly spelling out their disbelief. Those, however, who sincerely struggle to reach a belief but find it difficult because of their education and environment should not be held entirely responsible for it.

Our education and the standards by which other disciplines operate leave no room in our faculty of judgment for occurrences that cannot be subjected to the tests scientific logic employs for finding out the truth. But the scientific method is a way of finding out only that kind of truth which applies to the world of matter. And as far as that goes, the scientific method is, indeed, the best tool for making contact with and for living the kind of life material laws dictate to both nature and man.

This means that those who attempt to vindicate the

miraculous by employing syllogistic argumentations are not only laboring in vain but are liable to harm the cause of religion by implicitly restricting the latter's boundaries within the seen and measurable.

Our approach to the miraculous derives from a fundamentally different premise. This premise questions the supposition that there is nothing else in the cosmos apart from material forces in play with one another. A strong pointer to the belief that there are forces beyond and above matter is man's own mind as it constantly strives — and successfully so — to unravel the secrets of creation and to come in contact with energies that now are unknown because the human mind itself has not yet unravelled its own potentialities for knowing as much as it is ultimately capable of knowing.

Man's mind has already widened so much that it is impossible for any discipline to contain it within the world of material interrelationships. The proof to that is the fact that though we value truth deriving from factual experience and abide by it, we tend to tackle personal problems by whole personality attitudes rather than by strict logical argumentations. Hence, the most important decisions in our lives are seldom taken in strict compliance with logical data — as a computer would do — but on the strength of a considerable number of factors some of which we cannot even measure, let alone logically verify.

We tend, thus, to present two personae toward life: one fully permeated and utterly controlled by the procedure by which we come to know nature, that is, by the laws by which man's mind proves able to make sense out of phenomena; and the other, inexplicably and autonomously making decisions by virtue of which we deem ourselves to be enlightened and freed from material and tribal duress.

How can this be possible? Perhaps, because of the very nature of the human self as understood by Orthodoxy; as being a mixture of matter and mind in no definite proportions, as being a multiple of flesh and spirit with an implicit balance that cannot be disturbed by the one outweighing the other.

When the affairs of matter are under consideration, mental mechanics take over and require experiential data to fall into classifications of understanding apart from which reality cannot be conceived. These mental mechanics set the criteria of credibility and truth as regards material functioning. But when the self is involved in questions touching upon its own essence, a kind of primal sense takes over, a new tool of understanding, as it were. As a result, the individual finds a way to attune himself to situations that could not be grasped at all by way of rational means. This explains the fact that we are able to make decisions of capital importance on the strength of seemingly unknown factors but of the existence of which we seem to have no doubts.

The rationale and credibility of Christianity derive from this primal sense that we seem to possess and by virtue of which we grow certain regarding religious precepts that otherwise could not withstand the test of syllogistic scrutiny. Hence, our difficulties in invoking logic and proof as tools by which we can recruit others and convince them to believe as we do. Hence, also, the futility of trying to prove that miracles can be explained within the perimeter of the laws of nature.

Our spiritual anxiety seems to stem from a one-legged development of the human self. While man's mind has, indeed, advanced by leaps and bounds, this primal sense — someone called it the emotional self — has been left trailing at an appreciable distance. As a result, the mind and its tools and mechanics for recognizing the world have come to be accepted as the only media for discovering reality and scientific logic as the only criterion of truth.

But this one-legged development notwithstanding, the human self continues to seek the security of whole personality attitudes which, however, cannot be assumed without the primal sense contributing its findings. The clamoring for new symbols and new realities will continue fruitlessly until the individual re-establishes a balance in himself between the authority of mind and the inexplicable promptings of the primal sense.

All this means that man is not a computing machine which his mind can program and thereby have the answers to all questions that really bother him. Rather, the harmonious man is an all-inclusive entity the balance and wholesomeness of which depend upon an equilibrium between logical inevitableness and primal sense.

In a personality of this kind, reasoning and inner convictions interplay without leading either to rational dictatorship or to religious gullibility. Within this kind of personality, science can progress unimpaired by superstition and dogmaticism, and religion can instill its pristine dew without which no life is worth living. This is why we cannot prove the miraculous in our Faith and yet we can entertain it with that kind of sureness that generates harmony within, and impetus to higher planes of existence without.

Thus, the good news of the Annunciation becomes best news for those who do not seek to convince themselves about the scientific plausibility of the miraculous nor do they waste themselves in arguing the pros and cons of the legitimacy of religion in general. If their primal sense is sufficiently developed and has matured beyond the stage of credulity, they can develop a self which will be able to entertain in it both the thirst for knowledge of the tangible and the need for an inner attunement to realities far beyond the seen and observable. This is, apparently, the nature of faith for which Christ was asking: "Do you believe? Everything is possible for the one who believes."

For those who prove able to reach this kind of inner balance, not only parthenogeneses are possible but the breaking of the laws of nature on the part of the divine becomes a necessity for which the pure in heart have been asking since the beginning of human experience: "Let Thy Spirit come on us . . ."

American Orthodoxy

Orthodoxy was brought to North America by Russian missionaries and by way of Alaska. But missionary communities began to become transformed into immigrant communities as soon as Russian immigrants pushed down and into the United States proper mainly by way of the western coast. The strength of the Russian Church today, including all of its jurisdictional subdivisions, derives from the type of the community that developed within the United States as a minority Church: as a Church which, in a rather inhospitable environment, turned inwardly rather than out-wardly for the purpose of surviving as a distinct religious entity, not for the purpose of spreading her teachings and for recruiting believers from outside her national comple-ment and cultural atmosphere.

The Greeks, Romanians, Serbians, Syrians, Bulgarians, Albanians, Ukrainians, and Carpathorussians who followed, were faced with the very situation the Russians met with within the United States proper. The gradually forming communities were indirectly forced by the Protestant and Roman Catholic establishments around them to assume as religious communities the primary and singular aim of perpetuating their Faith and the way they practiced it within their own membership; a membership that was clearly delineated from the American environment of the time not only by way of articles of belief and worshiping practices but by way, as well, of the cultural environment within which their Faith was lived. This cultural environ-ment of theirs was in many respects in striking difference to that of the existing American socio-economic structure of the time.

This inward turning for the purpose of religious and cultural self-defense, grew gradually into a spiritual en-closure that became dangerously tight owing to the fact that most of the people and their clergy were pushed out of their native country for reasons of sheer poverty. This means that the average Orthodox immigrant — as most any other immigrant — lacked proper education, and the religious experience he brought with him was not, in many respects, representative of Orthodoxy as this was practiced in his country and within the more religiously enlightened element of his nation.

More than that, when he found himself in the midst of a strange and mostly inimical environment, he turned inwardly as regards his religion and as regards his national identification. His national identification yielded to him a way of thought and life that were dear to him and afforded him a considerable amount of emotional and mental security. Thus, nation and religion became fully amalgamated as regards his feelings, more so than they were in his native country where he was able to effect some kind of distinction between the two.

The first generation Orthodox Church in the United States served, then, the immigrant more than it hurt him by remaining a closed religious and cultural community. The fact that people sat tight as a group, even though within a kind of religious and cultural ghetto, was responsible for the second generation remaining Orthodox and for its being accorded an education much higher percentagewise than that which other groups afforded their children. The Orthodox immigrant plagued as he was with his destiny of manual labor — owing to his lacking education, language, and skill — swore that his children should not share his own fate in the new world. As a result, the majority of second and third generation Orthodox show a clear trend toward professions rather than business, that is, in the nature of the commercial establishments that a small percentage of first generation immigrants succeeded in establishing for themselves.

But all this is history, an array of personal annals filled with sweat and tears but successful nonetheless. Orthodoxy has been established in this country, but its original synthesis and narrow aims appear to have up to very recently resisted pressures from the American environment that it exit its spiritual and cultural enclosure and enter the American scene at large.

Present-day conditions, however, appear to demand a reorientation of the primary aims of Orthodoxy as a personal religion as well as a specific spiritual institution within the American life. The American Orthodox of today, having come of age as regards his personal religious experience and that of the group within which he moves, seeks a more definite and more convincing articulation of his Faith and a way of practicing it to which he could fully subscribe without hesitation or reservations and without fear of being severed on account of it from his American environment.

At the same time, he wants his Faith to be unveiled to the world, to be properly projected, and its points of excellence to be singled out as identification marks that would provide him with a secure place within the religious community of America. Our American born families, with an otherwise established position in the American society, want their Church to live the experience of the nation in its many-faceted adventure of search and progress.

Already, some important moves have been made toward this direction on the part of the Church, primarily in answer to explicit or implicit demands by congregations and their priests born outside the Orthodox countries. One of them relates to recapturing our place as a Church within the western world of religious experience, in fact, to confronting the rest of the Christian world with our identity as a Church the title to Apostolicity of which is second to none and whose claim to correctly believing can be substantiated by any means now available to theological research.

The first initiative of this kind was taken by the Ecumenical Partiarchate as long as forty years ago when it asked for the establishment of an ecumenical movement within Christianity at large. And when, finally, the World Council of Churches was established, the Ecumenical Patriarchate urged Orthodox participation with such vigor that some of the Orthodox national Churches resisted strenuously up to very recently, obviously, from fear for all non-Orthodox. Now, the World Council of Churches affords the Orthodox a kind of a world tribune from which not only his religious beliefs and his viewpoints on the problems of contemporary society can be injected to world opinion, but also his image can be successfully projected on the world scene, as this has been demonstrated by Archbishop Iakovos of the Greek Church during his tenure as one of the Council's presidents.

In another move purporting to disseminate Orthodoxy by way of theology, a team of theologians — primarily Russian — have made an important contribution toward bringing the essence of Orthodoxy not only to non-Orthodox but to many Orthodox as well who seek to understand Orthodoxy in a realm beyond the observable and customary.

Of course, the one event which brought Orthodoxy to the eyes of the world for the first time in our long history was the meeting between Patriarch and Pope. This gesture, apart from the concept of a world-wide brotherhood that it exhibited on our part, stirred up within the Orthodox Church an attitude of reappraisal of our own place within Christianity at large. The theology of reconciliation on the

94

strength of which this meeting was made possible, is in the nature of a call for searching our own Orthodox conscience. Also a testimony to the imperative need for restudying our own position and for reconstructing it, if necessary, on a contemporary foundation and in disregard to the past and its emotionally charged atmosphere.

Above all, the theology of reconciliation sounded a call for a general overhaul of our institutional structure and of the enactments of Councils that have regulated up to now our relations with non-Orthodox. For example, when the twenty years on the Patriarchal throne of our Ecumenical Patriarchate were celebrated in New York by an ecumenical doxology in which Catholic and Protestant prelates participated, a number of bishops from non-Greek jurisdictions issued a tactful condemnation of the fact that Archbishop Iakovos allowed non-Orthodox bishops to offer prayers during the service. Obviously, this did not only betray a viewing of the world reminiscent of things that happened a thousand years ago but it came to strengthen accusations from outside to the effect that Orthodoxy is insensitive to present-day reality, even to the essential purpose of Christianity which is the brotherhood of men.

Patriarch Athenagoras dragged the Orthodox, unwitting and unwilling, to the proscenium of world attention. By so doing, he did not only give a world identity to the Orthodox Church but charged the Orthodox with an unforgettable duty: to keep his Church alive, going, and progressing. For, an institution that exhibits an inability to adapt itself to the main stream of thought and life is bound to die out on the shelves of libaries. Those from among the Orthodox who find solace and personal self-fulfillment in the imperial atmosphere of Byzantium and Russia were, thus, asked to make room for contemporaries in whose mind and heart time does not stand still and in whose estimation one's obligations toward the present override romantic adherence to past glories.

It seems, however, that most Orthodox want progress for their Orthodox Church. But what kind of progress and how? Most of them view progress from the institutional viewpoint. There seem to be two schools of thought. The one urges: Americanize the Church. The other demands: unite all the Orthodox national jurisdictions into one. The motive, though, behind both of these requests seems to be the same; institutional strength and a vision of effecting an impact on the American scene.

To the understanding of most people, "Americanize the Orthodox Church," means to lighten Orthodox practices rather than beliefs by rejecting customs and ways of mass feelings and behavior that are culturally incompatible with the surrounding religious environment. Obviously, proponents of this call for Americanization object to Orthodox cultural overtones as these are found in each of the national jurisdictions.

Also, those who call for a united Orthodoxy in the form of a pan-Orthodox Church point out to the same problem; culture. What are we going to do with the cultural atmosphere by which each of the national jurisdictions feed their particular Church? Can a conglomerate of these cultural auras be created, acceptable to everybody, or should we get rid of all of them and leave Orthodoxy in the form of a religious skeleton that could guide the intellect but starve the emotions? The problem, then, is the cultural garment with which Orthodoxy is clad and which is often used as a substratum for our religious edifice to stand on. This means that before any kind of intelligent answer can be advanced to this predicament of ours, the nature, extent, and depth of the conjugation between Orthodoxy and the many cultures through which it is expressed in terms of religious experience must be honestly examined. The thesis by which our beliefs and practices have remained even to their most minute details genuinely Apostolic and Patristic is too precarious to even discuss. A brief going back to the beginnings of Christianity and then a following of Orthodoxy's acculturation to the present might help us to see clearer our present problem and, perhaps, enable us to reach a desirable solution.

The Acculturation of Orthodoxy

After St. Paul won a cosmopolitan purpose and label for the young Faith at the Council of Jerusalem over St. Peter's bid for Jewish acculturation, Christianity found itself culture-less and open to all kinds of cultural influences with which it subsequently came to contact. At the time, society was so culturally plurastic that a new group such as the Christian Church promulgating not only a new Faith but mainly a new way of life was bound to have a rough sailing in the midst of such cultural confusion.

Alexander the Great did not conquer all the way; he and his warriors submitted themselves to conquest, mainly by way of local culture and its pleasures. Alexander brought many things to the people he conquered, but he failed to bring them the highest form of the culture of that time, the Athenian way of life. Having stayed a barbarian at heart, he limited himself to transmitting a great deal of material culture, actually the culture he himself knew. His contribution to bringing a measure of the Greek spirit to non-Greeks was unintentional and only the result of his destroying the Athenian democracy. The spirit indwelling the Parthenon was chased out and southward to finally perch in its Hellenistic form in the city he built on the mouth of the Nile. But this non-material culture in the form of Hellenism was inaccessible to the first communities of the believers in Christ.

The Acts and the Epistles of the Apostles testify to the fact that the preachers of the new life in Christ met with a formidable opponent in the non-material cultures of the various people to whom they brought the Gospel. St. Paul himself had a difficult time in combatting cultural frames adverse to his preaching and was, on occasion, forced to compromise with some and even allow in some modified form the entry of others into the new religion.

As a result of this need for the Apostles to adapt existing cultural patterns to the framework of the Christian Gospel, Apostolic and sub-Apostolic Christianity acquired a multi-faceted cultural aura while at the same time proceeded with developing its own cultural articulation on the strength of the preached life in Christ. But then, rational attacks against the Gospel, either from within or without, afforded an unwitting opportunity to the apologists, both early and later, to bring the struggling Christian Church face to face with the non-material culture of Greece in its Alexandrine garment.

The apologists, especially the great ones of the Alexandrian school, found themselves in need of resorting to the intellectual panoply of Greek frames of thought and of employing the latters' methods of argumentation for the purpose of combatting a highly complex and dangerously plausible — at least on the surface — interpretation of the redemptory work of Christ; Gnosticism. Since the Gnostic interpretation of Christianity was supported from behind by an ingenius philosophical pragmatism, the apologists had to utilize to the fullest possible extent Platonic idealism in an attempt to counterbalance a theory of personal redemption that valued knowledge as the sole key to personal self-fulfillment. But by so doing, they introduced into the Christian precincts proper the main articulation of Greek philosophy from Sophistic solipsism down to Aristotelian scientific pragmatism.

Together with the necessary theoretical argumentation, they used a multitude of other frames of thought and a number of moral values emanating from the very heart of Athens, albeit dressed up with the kind of nebulous mysticism that was at the time overflowing the boiling kettle of Neoplatonism in Alexandria. The Gnostics, later the Arians and other heretics, were thus indirectly responsible for supplying Christianity with most of the elements of its non-material culture, at least for the time being.

The great Fathers who followed continued the work of defending the new Faith as heresies continued to spring up like mushrooms in a dump pile of humus. Their defense of that which was considered to be genuinely Apostolic became more intricate than that of the early apologists and more deeply drawing from Hellenistic learning. Their arguments of defense could withstand the most concentrated assaults of the intellectually skilled heretics and still leave a sizeable surplus of theological thinking on the basis of which the General Councils later built the dogmatics of our Christianity.

By the time Constantine issued his edict of freedom of religion, Christianity had acquired a non-material culture and that was primarily of Hellenistic origin. This kind of cultural substratum has never left Christianity in either East or West, primarily because it lies at the foundation of Christian belief as a supporting pillar without which Christian theology can easily turn into all kinds of religious personalism. If one adds to all this the help extended to Christianity by Stoic teachings and practices, one will have no difficulty in seeing that Christianity as we know it is — for better or worse — Hellenistic in its main articulation as an intellectual institution.

But in spite of all this, Christianity remained culture-less and still multi-cultured. Perhaps, because genuine Christianity cannot submit to any particular culture to the point of becoming fully identified with it, and yet it can coexist with many ways of living which a society can develop to meet its fundamental needs for survival, perpetuation of the species, and the ordering of social experience.

However, though applied Christianity is primarily a culture in itself, it cannot be absorbed by any kind of culture — as it never was — in spite of occasional beliefs on the part of certain Christian segments that true Christianity is exclusively theirs. The cultural soul of Christianity can absorb cultures, modify them, and re-express them by way of its own objectives and frames of reference. But at the same time, Christianity has allowed itself — this is very important — to be expressed by way of changing cultures. This, however, only for as long as the Church keeps the Gospel young and alive by trying to correctly read contemporary realities and produce ways of implementation that would befit the constantly changing human situation on earth.

Obviously, there is a strong vein of catholicity running through Christianity by which the latter can be unmistakably recognized and by virtue of which Apostolic preaching and practice still lie at the foundation of the genuinely christian Christianity. This, in spite of the accumulation of local color and tradition that gradually built up to the point of obscuring it. The Christian Churches appear at this time sincerely determined to penetrate the traditional for the purpose of reaching again this golden vein and of using it as the standard by which Christianity can be reunified inwardly as well as outwardly.

Eastern Christianity was not completely spared of events and developments of secular and temporal origin and scope and has not succeeded in retaining its primitive purity to the extent that we today realize it should have. This, not because Orthodoxy forsook its original clarity and genuiness; in fact, we believe it to be even in its many present-day cultural expressions truly Apostolic in essence and in its fundamental institutional structure.

It was the many peoples and the many nations that Orthodoxy was called upon to enlighten who forcibly identified it with their own particular personal and group objectives. Understandable as this may be on the sociological and psychological levels, Orthodoxy was nonetheless shaded by the thought and life of many peoples, in some respects to the extent of having become a tool for pursuing objectives to which the universality and apostolicity of Patristic thought would never have subscribed.

Christianity began to be subjected to international and interracial acculturation from the very moment St. Paul set his foot on Cyprus to begin his famous Apostolic Journeys. At that very time, the Jewish acculturation of Christianity — begun in Jerusalem primarily by St. Peter — was torn open for other cultures to get in. Mores, ideas, ideologies, remnants of former religious beliefs, customs, and social structures of the people converted, played a great part in contributing to what later developed to be our Christian culture.

This, because the Gospel the Apostles taught was not a complete social system dressed up in a cultural garment to the point of frills and fringes; rather, it was a Gospel of personal awakening to a new reality of thought, feeling, and doing, which, though, the individual himself had to make a way of life within a society imbued with a varying and, in most cases, self-contradicting past and present.

The average Christian proved unable, however, to perform such a gigantic personal reconstruction. Hence, early Christian communities found themselves in the midst of a culture in which Christian precepts were made to mix and cohabitate with pagan and Jewish beliefs and practices, often to their loss.

St. Paul's genius saw this all too well when he found himself compelled to communicate by letter with communities he had established, and established solidly as he thought at first. The old way of thinking and living and

102

the culture around the first Christian communities did not disappear as the newly baptized began to form Christian communities and attempted to live the new faith. Social and cultural environment, then as now, proved to be the most formidable adversary to the Apostolic teaching.

In answer to this threatening situation, St. Paul undertook to provide the Christian communities with a purely Christian nonmaterial culture, communities as far apart in spirit and locale as the east and west boundaries of the Roman empire were at the time. This work he continued to the very time of his death, thus laying the foundation of a Christian culture that was animated and defended by his own theological rationale which, in its turn, formed the foundation of Christian theology as we know it today.

But culture is carried by a social virus that sociologists still try to isolate with practically no results. It is not to be easily eradicated; it takes its course and always leaves a potentially explosive residue. Culture creeps up on people, and though no one appears to be singularly responsible for it, an imperceptible consensus of group will and whim grows to a massive attitude that no teaching to the contrary can change overnight.

This is the reason for which, as Christianity was in the process of growing in size and in inner strength, cultural parasites were growing up as well by feeding on it. The acculturation of Christianity that plagued the Apostolic age continued through the Byzantine era in the east and the Papal rule in the west, and still continues to function as the second leg of the Christian institution; a reality that many people resent today and count against the structure and practices of the Christian Church at large.

103

Culture played no insignificant role in the formation of the institutional structure of Christianity. Together with founding new Christian communities in the nature and composition of a Church, the Apostles were ordaining deacons and presbyters as officers and spiritual servants of local congregations to whom all matters of belief and practice should be referred for judgment and enforcement. But soon they found out that their Apostolic authority could not be vested in a pluralistic command. The communities continued to refer their questions, doubts, and quarrels to them personally. These were mostly of an organizational and practical nature related to problems of social structure and behavior more than to problems of pure belief, although problems of the latter nature were not infrequent. All of these, however, were indirectly related to problems of authority and command within the local church.

The idea of the office of the bishop — overseer — was to this time solely associated with the Apostles themselves who even from far away exercised their supervisory authority and served as the highest tribunal of reference in matters of both Faith and Order. But as the local churches were becoming more numerous and as they were proving unable to stabilize themselves within the perimeter of the Apostolic teaching as to Faith and the Apostolic direction as to Order — primarily because of being infiltrated by the surrounding culture and social structure — signs of separatism and surrender to non-Christian cultures were exhibited. The Apostolic presence in each one of them and at the right time proved problematic and nearly impossible, while the authority of the presbytery proved insufficient to hold together the local church as an organization avowed to pursue a spiritual end as high as that of the Christian Gospel.

Consequently, the Apostles — first of them St. Paul — saw the need of being present everywhere by an ordinant of theirs — the bishop — whom they invested with all the authority, rights, privileges, and duties they had ascribed to themselves. Thus, the office of the bishop was established which, though posterior to those of the deacon and presbyter, is indisputably of Apostolic origin.

Only a hundred years after the day of the Pentecost, the office and function of the bishop had been so deeply rooted in the esteem of the Church at large, that the bishop was considered to be the visible binding force of the Church, the supreme authority, and the only proof of the existence of a duly formed Christian community. The reasons for this pre-eminence of the episcopal office derive from the constant entanglement of the Christian Church with the nonmaterial culture within which the former was growing up and by which she was influenced while in the process of creating her own cultural motif by which she sought to supersede cultures that were besetting her.

However difficult this last task was to be — as it has proven to be by the survival to this very day of secular and in many respects inimical to Christianity cultures within the very Christian society — the Apostles realized from the very beginning that the Christian Gospel could not survive as a philosophical personal credo but only as a way of personal and group life in constant battle with folkways of thought and life deriving from non-Christian cultures. Hence, they were as particular about the teaching of the Gospel as they were about the order which the application of the Gospel should establish in terms of personal and group experience.

Hence also, the strong institutionalism that is characteristic of Christianity and the multitude of enactments on the part of Councils purporting to safeguard the Church's bid for a purely Christian culture. Thus understood, the Christian Church as a social institution can find a justification equally well defensible as that of any other social institution. And though the individual has suffered at the hands of institutional religion in a manner and extent that no one would expect from a religious institution, it was the super-zeal and lack of true spirituality on the part of clergymen that are responsible for this black mark for the Christian Church, not the institution as such.

Thus, as a result of this intensive care on the part of the Apostles and later of the Fathers to exclude from the Christian society all extraneous cultures, the Church grew gradually into a very closely knit institution with a monarchical system at its foundation. The Orthodox Church was spared of the monarchy at the top but gradually developed her own oligarchy. Some of us take pride in calling our Church democratic, but this should be understood to refer only upward from the office of the bishop. We do not have an absolute monarch at the top, all bishops being jurisdictionally equal. It is the synod of bishops in a national Church and all the bishops on the inter-Orthodox level that can deliberate and decide about the thought and life of the Orthodox Church at large.

But on the local level where the consciousness and conscience of the Church are formulated through time, the

Orthodox Church is governed by a monarch, the bishop. The bishop within his own jurisdiction is the absolute ruler with no court of appeal above him. This is a canonical prerogative, although national synods have gradually encroached upon this invulnerability of his. In countries where Orthodoxy is the state religion, the governing synod of the national Church may find an ally in the laws and powers of the state and may, need be, exercise a certain amount of effective control over the local bishop.

This brings us to the Byzantine era proper. The cultural battle in which the early Church found herself immersed continued unabated; if anything, it became intensified. This, because the Byzantine empire never ceased to be a conglomerate of nations and races with diverse cultures and educational backgrounds, save only one tradition that should perhaps be given priority, the Greek tradition. The Greek tradition was unquestionably excluded for being of pagan origin and irrespective of the fact that the Greek culture was deeply religious in essence and derived its strength from a theistic viewing of man and his environment. The virtues of a society that stand as a kind of model even for us today were ignored because of polytheism at its religious foundation. Some of the great Fathers of the Christian Church availed themselves of Greek learning by studying in Athens, but nothing more.

The Byzantine state and the Byzantine Church missed the opportunity of adapting to Christian patterns a culture that was still very much alive in the products of the Greek mind from art and public life to literature and philosophy. This is the reason for which Greece remained the glory that was, and though the language of Byzamntium finally became

Greek, its personal and public life together with its culture remained non-Greek, uncultivated and confused. The great men of Byzantium, churchmen and otherwise, flourished in spite of their environment, while the great men of Greece merely reflected the spiritual and cultural caliber of the society of their time. In the former case, greatness was a phenomenon, in the latter, it was a logical product of time and environment.

Neither was Byzantium Roman in any way apart from its jurisprudence. Its cultural substratum was pluralistic to the point of being disorderly. The state, the Church, the spiritually elite, all failed to provide a culturally adhesive force that could hold the nation together not by a mercenary army and by trade but by way of a deeply rooted national conscience and consciousness on the strength of which alone peoples survive with an identity of their own.

Byzantine culture — being a little more than the effects of cultural clashes at the crossroad between east and west — was fundamentally and predominantly materialistic in spite of its semblance of being strongly theocratic. Its theocracy was most of the times a mere instrument for power at the hands of secular or religious leaders, while the state's true power derived from the Byzantine military and mercantile genius and the way of pleasurable life it produced for the ruling class from the emperor down to the mercenary soldier and the local civil servant. The proof to that is that when barbaric hordes finally succeeded to block Byzantium's commercial outlets, the state as such ceased to exist and the empire got dissolved into its many dissimilar components.

How did Orthodoxy fare through all this? Pretty well,

considering the fact that for most of the time it was so closely associated with the state — mostly by force on the part of the latter — that it was compelled to follow its fortunes. Not that churchmen did not play the politicians or politicians did not become churchmen for the purpose of controlling the Church. But all in all, Orthodoxy's casualties as a result of its identification with the state, the aims of which were only pretentiously religious, did not exceed those that other segments of Christianity suffered under similar circumstances.

Orthodoxy's great battle during the Byzantine era was fundamentally cultural. First, the application of the Apostolic teaching in the form of an organized Church with a gradually developing ritual clashed with non-Christian attitudes and practices that were brought in as a result of the massive christianization at the time of Constantine. Then, fundamental precepts of Biblical origin were put to doubt and extraneous teachings deriving from pagan backgrounds crept in; these, the Church could not accept.

The Church proved eminently successful in fighting the new teachings, now known as heresies, but a cultural infiltration of Orthodoxy — as regards both material and non-material culture — could not be fully stopped. This, because the environment of the empire was as pluralistic culturally as Greece was polytheistic religiously. This was reflected in the ritual of the Church and its underlying customs and ideologies. And though the ritual was constantly under revision, a number of non-Christian mentalities, attitudes, and practices, deriving from pagan or Jewish cultural storehouses are still with us.

A careful reader of the Canons of both General and local

Councils will have no difficulty in seeing that by far the greatest number of Canons deal with mores, customs, and personal practices betraying an origin other than Christian. The reader will be appalled by the immorality and lower cultural personal and group practices to which the Canons testify. This might be a consolation to those who believe that we live today the most dissolute and most corrupt stage of human development on earth. Apparently, society was as diseased then as it is now.

In some instances, even the Canonical facing of these problems leaves much to be desired from the viewpoint of purity in Christian living. Corrective measures appear to aim at suppressing the symptoms rather than at eradicating the cause. At times, one has the feeling that the Church instead of defeating non-Christian cultures was herself captured by them.

The cultural invasion of Apostolic Orthodoxy can also be traced by a brief examination of Orthodox monasticism. Monasticism in the nature of a massive exodus from society by which it has become associated with Orthodoxy is a much later development; in fact, it appeared much after the great Fathers had in Council and in theology crystallized the essence and boundaries of Orthodoxy.

Monasticism in one form or another is not a Christian innovation. Both, monastic brotherhoods and hermits existed in the East much before Christianity. Byzantine monasticism, however, is peculiar because of its close association with the state of society from which it derived. When the community of Mount Athos was established, it attracted people from all walks of life, from emperors to shepherds, from Patriarchs to deacons; it attracted people with an inward urge to flee society and its vicissitudes. Admittedly, society at the time had little to offer to people sensitive to the realities of seeking personal development in reference to the overall principle of being we call God.

Yet Byzantine monastics were driven by a philosophy of life that can hardly be traced in the Bible or in Apostolic tradition. It rather derived from religious practices that can be traced to Judaism and through it to a personal conviction of oriental origin regarding the futility of social life and the impossibility of a spiritually inclined individual to live in it productively. This conviction was obviously the result of the rapid rise and fall of empires in Asia Minor and Mesopotamia and of the spiritual havoc they played with their coming and passing in the hearts and souls of religiously sensitive individuals. The great movement of Stoicism at about the same time, reflected the same awakening of the individual to the inherent moral fiber and potentialities of personal life as against the totalitarian and secular aims of the state.

Eastern monasticism — as against its development in the West — remained to the end fundamentally contemplative with little or no social import. It was exclusively the business of the individual and for the individual, and whatever benefits spilled over to the society were incidental and indirect. Its philosophy was one of rejecting evil in society, but together with its evil it rejected society as such and thus failed to recognize the inherent goodness in people and work for it. This type of theoretical and egocentric solitariness, obviously constituted a selfish viewing of man and his cosmos in spite of the self-denial code that it imposed on its membership. Instead of being used as a means to an end, in the example of our Lord's retreats for inward strengthening, it became an end in itself. But as soon as social conditions began to change for the better after the industrial and other revolutions, this kind of monasticism began to decline.

This does not mean, however, that our type of monasticism did not serve our Orthodoxy. It did serve it, and served it well, especially when both state and Church were fighting for their lives. Whenever society reached the lowest possible ebb of its moral fortitude and proved unable to regenerate itself, our monastic communities did shine their inward light to illuminate the path of return for both Church and state. And when the state ceased to exist as such and its people were subjugated to non-Christian invaders, our monastic communities acted not only as treasury vaults for our Faith and Tradition but as cells, as well, of spiritual resistance that in time generated the needed force for liberation. Strange as this may appear to be, eastern monasticism came really of age whenever Church and nation were faced with extinction. When society was functioning normally, monasticism fled both its evil and its goodness, but when the people were fighting for their lives and their values, monasticism found a way to prove of inestimable social service.

Obviously, the future Orthodox monasticism will by circumstances and current conditions become oriented more toward society than toward itself. Monasticism as such will survive all kinds of cultures because it does answer the need of certain types of personality for an introverted higher type of experience. It can become abnormal, though, when its inward solitariness generates in the individual a rejection of his intellectual and spiritual environment. When prayerful meditation and inward enlightenment are radiated outwardly and are translated into concrete contributions to man's material and spiritual well-being, monasticism — whether one lives in a monastery or not — can counterbalance powerful influences in society that push people to a life of nothingness.

Let us now follow the acculturation of our Orthodoxy as it spread north of Byzantium. The missionaries who took Orthodoxy to the rest of the Balkan peninsula and then to the greatness and vastness of Russia, did not take with them a dogmatical skeleton and a prescribed way of life that would answer the requirements of a dry list of religious norms. They brought to those people a religious atmosphere rather than a rational articulation of an altogether new faith the understanding of which would normally require an acquaintance not only with monotheism but with Greek patterns of thought as well.

By instinct or by wisdom, Saints Cyril and Methodius, together with their collaborators and successors, introduced the Slavs to Orthodoxy by way of an emotional and cultural religious spectrum, the extent, depth, and glitter of which proved to be highly effective in tutoring those young and vigorous people to Christianity by the door of Byzantium. And about that time, Byzantine Orthodoxy had reached the apogy of its aesthetic development by way of literature, art, music, and ceremonial riches. The mystical atmosphere, lacking in the early Church, had by now become so overpowering that it had taken over Church life almost completely. It is a matter of wonder whether an early Church type of Orthodoxy would have taken roots north of

113

Byzantium, considering the fact that it would have required a certain level of personal and group development to be understood and a certain degree of inward discipline to be practiced in its clear but dry logical articulation.

Be that as it may, Byzantium's psychological approach — even unwittingly — found a very fertile soil, and Orthodoxy spread quickly to develop and even pitch its acropolis in Russia when later the Turks overran the Byzantine empire. Perhaps, some of the most important reasons for Orthodoxy taking roots so deeply among the Slavs include: the concept of the emperor-bishop, the concept of the bishop-emperor, and the mystical concomitants of the faith and order that afforded the masses a very personal involvement and would help them exit, need be, the oppression of their feudalistic governments and fulfill themselves in the intangible world of religion.

Soon, Orthodoxy became a very serious preoccupation with the Slavs precisely as it was with the Byzantines. Not that this preoccupation was in its entirety of a truly religious nature. Vested political, economic, cultural, and personal interests, warred within society at the expense of Orthodoxy in the pattern of the Byzantine infights — in some cases even worse. The emperor-bishop proved to be the protector of faith and Church but nonetheless their tyrant. The bishop-emperor behaved within the perimeter of his privileges in exactly the manner of the emperor-bishop and second only to him. The congregation turned — or was turned — to a religious experience predominantly emotional and mystical in nature. As a result of this, people entered a state of being highly susceptible to religious credulity and as they became immersed deeper and deeper into the arts that developed around the religious core of Orthodoxy, they tended to confuse political and social gospels with the Gospel of Christ.

A religious situation of this kind issued, of course, in a further acculturation of Orthodoxy. The more outwardly the stress was laid the closer the Church was brought to the hearts of the people and the deeper her life was influenced by cultural modes, racial traits, and national fortunes. The mystical trend of Byzantine Orthodoxy was not only well received but extensively cultivated and strongly expressed in both theological thought and liturgical practice.

The liturgical articulation and practice of the Church underwent a significant embellishment so as to fit the emotional and behavioral patterns of the people. Music and church decor followed the cultural development of the people concerned, and art and architecture imperceptibly exhibited the psychogenic characteristics of Slavic people and their particular ecological, social, and political realities as their nations were growing into political and social powers of their own. Their subsequent ecclesiastical emancipation from the Mother Church in Constantinople added an autonomy to them not only in letter but primarily in spirit and diverse development.

Significantly, the theology of the Slavic segment of Orthodoxy predominantly expresses and furthers the symbolic and mystical realities of personal religion. Although it does not ignore the Church as an establishment, it is not a consolidating type of theology as the one following the Schism and still prevalent among Greek and other theologians. The most representative Russian theologians of the last few centuries are of the philosopher-theologian type who is moved to reflection on the substratum of a system of metaphysical idealism the object of which is the individual rather than the group. This kind of theology is, of course, fundamentally mystical and expressive of the search for a personal religious experience of the highest order.

Such, in the main, has been the acculturation of Orthodoxy through the ages and through the many peoples it has been assigned to serve and tutor to Christ from the time St. Paul preached on the Areopagus to our present-day Orthodox religious conglomerate.

Unified American Orthodoxy

Obviously, the Orthodox Church in America is still heavily conditioned by its underlying culture, a culture that is pluralistic and in many respects so diverse as to have kept up to now the various Orthodox Churches in a friendly estrangement to one another.

A considerable segment of the congregations of all Orthodox Churches press for a united Orthodox Church not only for reasons of social import and a stronger voice in our American society, but for important practical considerations. One of these reasons that grievously concerns Orthodox parents is marrying their children within their own faith.

Orthodox parents who take their religion seriously wish to marry their children within their own faith. But the present lack of communication between the memberships of the Orthodox Churches deprives the youth of the opportunity and chance to marry within their Orthodox Church. As laymen, they cannot see why the Orthodox Churches could not have a unified command, and think and act as one body that they dogmatically are. This would open the door for inter-church mixing and could afford the opportunity to people to establish a religious and social bond within their own faith, even if outside their own national origin.

Orthodoxy in America is indeed in danger of being dogmatically and culturally levelled off and of ultimately being effaced by absorption. This danger might not appear real to some of us today, but a long view of the past and present does not warrant an optimistic prediction. For one, what are today national jurisdictions will cease to be so, perhaps by the time the next generation takes over. If the cultural overtones underlying the Faith are not distilled and the truly Orthodox ones intentionally preserved, Orthodoxy will be gradually stripped of its cultural flavor by which it is mainly distinguishable from other sacramental Churches. And though few, if any, will lament the severance of the American Orthodox Churches from the influence of the countries of their origin, nobody will afford to rejoice at the loss of the cultural overtones of any Orthodox Church here.

Can a unified command remedy this situation? No, if things stand as they are. A jurisdictional union should come only as a result of cultural and liturgical clarification. And it is at this area that the leaderships of the various jurisdictions should start working. For the American born Orthodox, the existing liturgical and cultural diversity is something he cannot comprehend and a definite impediment toward having a unified Orthodox congregation that could be at home in any Orthodox church. Churchmen should bear in mind that the young want definite and undoubted situations if they are to really belong to the Church. Also, that they are not prepared — nor will they ever be — to accept customs and mores that are not only passe but run against the grain of true Orthodox beliefs. And situations such as these abound in all jurisdictional Churches.

Obviously, each national Church should seriously and earnestly begin to clean her house culturally and ceremoniously. The fact that many absurdities are customary and are called traditional should not deter the authorities from discerning their incompatibility with the essence of Orthodoxy. Also, the fact that people feel safe and secure because of such a long association with them should not prevent the latters' rejection. And though the Orthodox dislike to admit that there are Churches from which they should learn, the historic job of the Vatican Synod should lend them courage to assume responsibilities that are theirs, not of the coming generation.

After this cultural shifting is over, the remaining cultural overtones should be bound together on the basis of a truly Orthodox denominator and be offered for observance to all Orthodox Churches. Customs and practices characteristic of particular Churches should be respected and preserved insofar as they do not come up against the pan-Orthodox sense of genuiness. Varying customs and practices that can be reconciled should be amalgamated by agreement of the Churches concerned. All this is not an easy task, but one that has to be tackled.

Then, each Church should critically examine her liturgical life for interpolations and whimsical changes through the centuries owing to causes other than religious. And we have to admit that the ritual, as beautiful as it is, requires a considerable amount of editing. Its sacred character is not going to fly away if it is rendered fit for today's worshipping congregations.

Those who take the ritual to be untouchable should bear in mind two things: first, it has never stood static during the golden age of Orthodox theology. Our very liturgies underwent extensive changes till they were given their present form which, at any rate, does not appear to be a final one. The Fathers did not consider the ritual untouchable, as it is clearly evidenced by their rearrangements of the liturgical material and by adding to it their own compositions. The tragic part of the development of our ritual is the fact that together with our great Fathers lesser theologians, who would have today a hard time to get even a bachelor's degree in theology, appended their own poor compositions and these survived through the ages as part and parcel of the truly good ones.

Second, we should bear in mind that the Orthodox prove extremely concerned and touchy if something is left out of their ritual, but no one complains when seemingly pious but nonetheless offensive additions are contributed by monastics whose ambition cannot be matched by the end-product of their inspirations. After the great stars of Orthodoxy had set, a considerable number of pious monks played the theologian and the poet to the great loss of our whole ritual, sacraments and all other services.

It is strange that though the Church does allow even today new material to go into our ritual, she remains adamant as regards a revision and editing of it. For example, in the last few years the Church of Greece has sanctioned commemorative services for newly canonized saints who were practically our contemporaries. The Russian Churches of America only a few months ago decided to honor as a saint an Alaskan missionary and, no doubt, a church service will be composed in his honor for public worship. There is nothing wrong with these actions. At least, we show that we are an alive Church and saintliness and sainthood dwell among us as of old.

But the same loving care should be extended to us living. Prayer and worship make up the epitome of faith and practice. Praying is fundamentally an action of petitioning God. But what do we petition for? The great majority of our petitions have to do with material commodities and natural occurrences. But today's congregations do not need to pray for outward material conditions but for inward realities. The problem of man has been shifted from God's nature to the nature of man. Nature is by now well under man's control, and before long even entire climates will be changed to the benefit of man. But the inward climate of man remains just as violent as it was at the very beginning. It is for favorable inward climatic conditions that we should pray.

The various national Orthodox Churches in this country can never become truly united unless each one of them clarify their present cultural and ceremonial situation; that is, unless we produce by a courageous critical study, commensurate to our responsibilities toward the coming generations, a meaningful and truly Orthodox cultural and ceremonial compedium. This, for the young to appraise in their minds and hearts and discover for themselves the value and worth of particular traditions and the desirability and feasibility of their being preserved. Then, a ceremonial uniformity should be worked out by the leaderships of the various Churches to the extent that an American born Orthodox will be at home at any service performed by any Orthodox priest. The unified command, perhaps in the form of a ruling Synod, will follow naturally.

We need a Prayer Book for Today's Orthodox

Orthodox worship, as any other Christian or even pagan worship, may be viewed and examined both as personal and as common worship. The act of worship as such is an attempt on the part of the believer or believers to communicate with their particular deity by means of one way dialogue for the purpose of effecting desired changes in his or their experience; worshiping acts, though, for the sole purpose of saying *thanks* to God are neither infrequent nor less genuine.

Worship is actually a prayer or a series of prayers with a certain and definite meaning that leaves no doubt as to its purporting to bridge the finite with the infinite, the human with the divine. This intent is further carried out by worshiping acts the purpose of which is to illustrate the words and allow the worshipper not only to act out the content of the prayer but to live it out as well in terms of personality states that would at the time fully dominate his waking consciousness.

A worshipper can, thus, live moments that are clearly

beyond the capacity of his ordinary inner self and can enter a higher level of existence even if it is only for the duration of his worship. Or, a worshipper can utter words and go through the motions of offering himself to his worshipful master and still remain inwardly unmoved for no fault of his own; merely, because the type and content of worship failed to arouse in him the urge to do away with his worldly preoccupation and to surrender himself entire to the power of the Spirit he desires to establish contact with.

This brings in the question of the nature and format of our personal worship as viewed and experienced by the average Orthodox; not by the insensitive and indifferent, or the exceptionally gifted who needs little or no prompting for reaching a higher state of religious experience. The average Orthodox whom we should have in mind is the one who desires elevation and is susceptible to tutoring in the ways of Christ and to being led into the aura of our Orthodoxy. He is the future of our Church and the future of Orthodoxy, the seeker of sense in everything that he does or is done for him; the one who wants to become partaker in the life of Christ and of the life of the Church, not to remain an onlooker as he is most of the times condemned to. It is, then, not so much the mentality and the approach that some of us seek to change so that today's congregations could be offered a share of our beliefs and practices; rather, it is the question how personally significant our beliefs and practices can prove for this average Orthodox. Nothing less than an undoubted relevance to the needs and wants of his soul and mind will do.

But let us, briefly, examine the nature and format of personal worship. Personal worship is an act of presenting ourselves before our own image of God for purposes that may vary on occasion but on the strength of an implied relationship between us and God as we understand Him. The occasions for which the individual may seek contact with God may vary widely and so his personality states may range just as widely, from begging to thanksgiving, and from guilt-depression to a feeling of inner self-fulfillment.

Underlying the whole spectrum of motivation for contacting God is the felt understanding on our part that He and we are in some kind of bond on the strength of which we have the right to call on Him. This inward sense of being related to God generates in us a conviction of strength that derives from beyond and in spite of our own powers and settles in the back of our minds as a sense of being rooted in another world, a fact by virtue of which alone we can live in this one. This mute sense of derivation from and affiliation with God is called divine sonship, and it is on the conviction of this relationship that personal worship is possible as a meaningful offering of one's soul to the loving care of God.

Thus, the foundation of personal worship rests on a sense of implied relationship to God, and, as a result, on an absolute surrender of the individual's mind and soul to Him that He may strengthen and guide them. And though telling God the particular reason for calling on Him is obviously unnecessary, personal worship is also personal drama and one's soul must lighten itself of its burden by thinking aloud the rationale of its failures or the logic of its petitions. The heart must be cleansed of conflicting motivations and colliding impulses. The self must convince itself of the legitimacy of its viewing itself with the proper measure of self-esteem. All this and much more is called confession, that is, self-emptying in front of a superior power believed to be motivated toward the worshipper by love which, however, He can grant or withhold. And since withholding love generates punishment, the individual stands before God in love and in judgment.

This is the point where personal worship becomes identified with personal prayer, if the content and format of prayer are truly representative of the states of mind and heart of the individual in dialogue with God. And this is the point where the Church has the obligation to see that the Christian in need of communication with God is given the proper help and the means by which to adequately express himself through prayer.

Worship and personal prayer are religious experiences that are not unique to us in any way. Thus, we cannot refuse to answer the needs of our congregations on the excuse that an Orthodox prayer does not have to be that specific as long as it provides the traditional emotionality, atmosphere, and that mystical air that generates from the unintelligible ceremonial murmur of the traditional Orthodox priest. Our people feel the need to pray for themselves and we are duty bound to teach them the way as well as to supply them with the subject-matter of their desired discourse with God, seeing that an individual who finds himself compelled from within to bend his soul before his Maker is in a sacred and extremely important personality attitude. Personal prayer is indicative of the condition of one's spiritual health and the only substratum on which one's inner temple can rest.

We are in need of an Orthodox collection of personal

prayers designed to answer our own particular needs in our own particular environment; commensurate to our own standards of education, our scientific understanding of the world, and our technological viewing of life. We have no personal prayers that could express the thinking, needs, problems, and the yearning of the average member of our congregation or could effect the serenity and surety that prayer representative of one's inner fiber can generate in our hearts.

We need a prayer book that could become not only the spiritual possession of the contemporary Orthodox but his manual as well by which his heart, his mind, and his mouth could be opened and effect thereby his acquaintance with God. We have no prayers with this individual in mind, or, for that matter, with any individual at all. Apart from emotionally purgative prayers written for the individual to recite before he goes to Holy Communion, the rest of our prayers that deal with the individual's problems of every day life have nothing to do with the individual. The reason? They have been written for the group, but for a group with which we are not even acquainted today. All of our prayers have monastic brotherhoods in mind and the conditions of their daily living and routine, their temptations, and their philosophy of life; a philosophy of life, though, which we cannot accept today owing to its negative attitude toward plain human living believed to be potentially devilish and destructive of the soul. But viewing life from this angle would tend to convince us that the best thing we can do to keep our life pure is to pray for its termination lest we fall prey to the machinations of the devil who is allegedly after us.

Accordingly, the mental set one is expected to assume is one of watchfulness against evil spirits and evil people. This watchfulness, though, is bound to generate in one's soul a conviction to the effect that this world is fundamentally and inescapably evil and our presence in it is the result of sin, a kind of sin from which we can hardly redeem ourselves. Faith in the goodness of the human heart is lacking and personal relationships are thus practically impossible on any basis whatsoever. This kind of theology by which the worthlessness of man is stressed more than his talent to redeem himself through Christ leaves little room for personal hope and personal improvement.

In addition, practically every prayer is a dogmatical statement for which people can have hardly any use today since we are not at war with heretics. This constant preoccupation with doctrinal infights has robbed our few prayers — that could be used in earnest and in private — of the human touch and the human cry for God's hand to reach us and heal us.

Another unnecessary preoccupation that plagues most of our personal prayers has to do with sexual morality. For today's reader, this identification of morality with the sexual ethics of the time is historically and culturally interesting but little more than that. We know by now that one's moral behavior does not begin and end with sexual behavior; rather, it is conditioned and controlled by forces and factors reaching farther than cultural regulatory standards of sexual behavior. The true temptations of life extend much beyond sexual primitiveness to include the very heart and soul of man whereform one's attachment to persons and beliefs derives. And we have found out that the quality of the attachment that the individual will finally cement with the world via the people is the determining force that will make him moral or immoral. If temptation could be solely contained within man's sexual desires, the problem of evil would not be as formidable as it is, seeing that today we are in a position to chemically control or completely alleviate sexual temptation.

It is extremely unfortunate that in spite of the spirit of Orthodoxy — more personal than collective — our prayers appear to ignore the individual in preference to the brotherhood or nation. And the Byzantine Church, in spite of its power, proved unable to prevail over monasticism and its implied enmity toward the family notwithstanding the latter's obvious importance for the survival of the Church. And though there was a clear separation between monastics and parochial clergy, it was the former's prayers and directory of worship that finally prevailed. We still find ourselves reciting personal and communal prayers either in private or in public worship that were composed for monks and brotherhood worship.

This has all along prevented the lay Orthodox from really participating in the regenerative act of Christian worship, and as church services became through the centuries more and more involved in poetry, dogmatical exposition, and music, and as they drew longer and longer in duration, the average lay Orthodox finally became an onlooker instead of a wholehearted participant. The only situation to which he succeeded to hold on is a kind of emotional upheaval generated by the whole atmosphere of monastic worship, by the awe inspiring environment, the outworldliness of our syncopated music, and the air of a mystery that shrouds things said and done within the Orthodox temple. True, this personal situation has proved beneficial for the average Orthodox considering that by it one's heart could be purged, even temporarily, from the turbulence of worldy conflicts, and a kind of emotional security could be afforded as a result of one's clinging to the outward form of worship.

It is this feeling of being in the midst of an outworldly performance that is responsible for the traditional piety of the average Orthodox. But since this kind of piety is mostly limited to awe for the objects, the symbols, the words, the actions, the sounds, and the whole spectrum of visual and auditory stimuli in our worship, it does not necessarily involve the worshipper any more than it would a spectator; so, its value to one's religious experience is strictly personal. Still, many Orthodox have anchored themselves on worship and on a diffused sense of personal sanctification they seem to derive from it, as if these could be the epitome of a personal religion of the highest order. Orthodoxy does not seem to be a religion for them but a deeply moving religious experience produced and directed for them by highly skilled artists and artisans. Needless to say, this kind of outward piety proves unable to support the heart when the storm of life chances to beat on it as on a solitary reed in an open field. The fault is not theirs!

Fortunately or unfortunately, we in this country can produce for our people neither the spectacle nor the experience that the Church used to produce in the past. Our churches are not in semidarkness, and the mysterion and mystique of the environment by way of art and music are gradually resolving to a clarity reminiscent of ancient Greek simplicity rather than of the emotional, aesthetic, and artistic complexity of Byzantium and its times. But since we cannot produce — we would not want to even if we could — the emotional supports for the outward piety of past generations, we have to bring our people into the true sacred precinct of Orthodox faith and worship by making them active participants of the mysterion and mystique of the drama of our Orthodox worship.

For this, we are in urgent need of methods and tools by which the contemporary Orthodox can have his Orthodoxy changed from a pedantic dogmatical exposition and a liturgical pageant to a personal involvement of the most serious and most rewarding nature; then, dogma could become a meaningful guide in believing and the liturgical mystery could effect an inner baptism to an experience that would extend beyond reason but without ignoring or violating its principles.

As for personal prayer, this has to be concrete and has to deal with the person's interests, dreams, fears, guilts, and hopes for the future; not because God has to know, as if He did not, our affairs in narrational detail but because the individual has to listen to himself and see himself talking to God. The emptying out of one's inner state in the presence of God affords the individual a sense of innermost relief that springs from the very realization that God his Father is witnessing his drama and, in a way, is sharing his passion. At this point, prayer becomes personally meaningful and personally important as a recourse to one's own depths to find therein the divine solace and guidance one cannot generate for himself. But this type of wondrous prayer has to deal with the individual, not with the generalities of personal experience as seen by others.

Obviously, our existing prayers do not view the individual as possessing the value and worth that we believe he does, so much so that Orthodoxy is fundamentally conceived and developed with the individual rather than the group in mind. Today more than ever before, personal religious experience requires reassurance and fortification while its counterpart in the form of institutional church practices goes through such a severe crisis.

For centuries, we have been supposedly fighting for the Church — that is, for the people of God — but our fights instead of having helped the people have added estrangement and division on division. It is about time for theology to stop chasing phantoms, return home, and vindicate its lofty name in the esteem of modern man; show how beneficial to the simple Christian it can prove, not as a spokesman *ex cathedra* but as a servant of the intellectual and spiritual yearning of people to attach themselves to an all-embracing principle from which we want to derive and to which we want to return. The Orthodox Church in America has considerable resources in talent and brain power. But most of it is now wasted, unoriented, aimless, and in complete oblivion of the needs of the Church. The concept of the Orthodox theological theoretician in the pattern of the proletarian theoretician should be abandoned, and the Church should give assignments of a definite and utilitarian nature to all of her theologians. True Patristic thought was never expended in theory for its own sake and irrespective of some important personal and communal practice in the life of Christ. Aimless theologizing is characteristic of the decline period of the Orthodox reasoning about God and man.

Liturgical Reform

A liturgical reform will not effect miraculous changes in the Orthodox world nor will it safeguard Orthodoxy's survival on the now constantly and violently shifting Christian substratum. This last will be decided in conjunction with the whole idea of organized religion as a cultural value, an idea that has yet to undergo its most severe testing during the coming decades when our present youth mellow and begin to wrinkle within the confines of marriage and family.

However, a liturgical reform — as extensive and as well-appraised as contemporary conditions may require — will help immensely both clergy and laity by allowing people to assume the experience of Orthodoxy as their own personal concern instead of viewing it, as now, from the standpoint of the admirer and member only by baptism. That worn-out noun *participation* will finally become meaningful to people, at least, as meaningful as they want it to be, and it may be that for many this will be the first time that they might catch themselves personally involved in the liturgy instead of just witnessing its performance from the safety and neutrality of their pews. We are not going to cite texts and discuss details. But from that which we are going to discuss, our need for talking to God as a Church in a language that derives from our hearts and expresses our present-day viewing of the world and ourselves will become more than apparent.

Few can perhaps realize that our real problem at this stage of our development is not which tongue we should use in our worship, English or any other, but what do we mean by that which we express; whether the substance, not merely the form, of our worship is supremely meaningful to us as it should be. This, because of the fact that worship is man's way of communicating with God and as such reflects the individual's and the group's development through the ages in their understanding of God and of themselves. This means that a liturgical reform should not be limited to form and language but it should be primarily concerned with and reflect the thought and personality attitudes of contemporary Orthodox as regards the problem of human placement within the world of matter as well as within the world of spirit.

All this has come to the surface now that we are under pressure to produce English translations. In many cases, the translation sounds not only flat but as a mere aggregate of words that lacks inner cohesion and that kind of meaning that would ring a bell down deep in the heart and soul of today's worshipper. This lack of contemporaneousness is apparent but only to specialists due to the fact that our liturgical language has ceased to be a spoken language and its antiquity has shielded texts that otherwise would have been edited long ago were the language fully understood and inwardly felt by the people.

There are but few services out of the whole range of our ritual that are directly and personally concerned with the people as individuals. Of the sacraments, baptism with confirmation, penance, Communion, and marriage, are actually the ones that bring the individual to a personal confrontation with his organized religion and require him to take a position within this sacred perimeter we call the Church. But though these services require the individual to take a position, yet they do not allow him to fully make his

132

own the experience they are supposedly intended to convey; this, by ignoring him as a person with reasoning powers of his own, with an emotional make-up of his own, with an intelligence of his own, and with a level of personal cultivation all of his own.

Our services, whether sacraments or other kind of ritual, seem to take the individual in a nonindividual manner much like in the manner of the individual-group identification in the city-state concept of ancient Greece. The priest, even when performing for the sole benefit of a certain individual acts on behalf of the whole Church, as an agent of the whole complement wherefrom his authority derives. In so doing, he follows certain predetermined steps by which the Church is through him exercising her rights as the indisputable treasury and dispenser of the Grace. Conditions of dispensing the Grace are set by the Church through the priest, and the rationale behind all things said and done is supplied by the Church while the recipient of the Grace remains passive and silent.

All this is fine, apart from one thing; the recipient of the sacrament is supposed to be in full accord with every implicit and explicit statement and meaning expressed and meant by the celebrant and his actions. And in theory he is, but very seldom in practice. The ritual itself does not allow the priest to find out whether the recipient of the sacrament agrees with the conditions under which the sacrament is dispensed by the Church; nor can the question of the recipient's spiritual attachment in general be ascertained one way or another since from the beginning to the end of the sacrament he stands there in the role of a mute witness. The same talking and acting on the part of the

Church is characteristic of all sacraments save penance in which, however, few of the recipients really talk.

Did the Church want to keep people silent at such important moments of their lives? Is this an unwarranted spiritual guardianship on the part of the Church for the purpose of preventing the people from having a say implicitly or explicitly in spiritual matters? An unwarranted spiritual guardianship it is, but not for the purpose of spiritually oppressing the people to keep them ignorantly obedient; rather, because at the time our ritual was in the process of being crystallized people,were not in a position to think for themselves along these lines, let alone speak for themselves. The Church was their guardian in thought and in action and they were, as they should be, grateful for that, although some claim that it was the State and the Church that kept people incapable of thinking for themselves. Be that as it may, this kind of arrangement can hold up no more.

The average individual of today is in a position to think out our religious theses, he is in a position to understand the rationale of our theology — apart from some wild abstractions and conjectures that nobody in his right mind could understand — and he is in possession of an aesthetic criterion by which he can judge both the form and the performance of our ritual. But above all, he has a philosophy of life, a viewing of this temporal experience that is all his own and by which he measures for his own benefit the utility and productivity of the spiritual guardianship we offer him by way of the sacramental life of the Church. He cannot be ignored as the recipient of a sacrament because it is on the strength of his willing powers that the sacrament will fruit or not. Furthermore, it is his religious philosophy and the latter's substantiation in terms of ecclesiastical practices that will decide not only the nature of the Church of tomorrow but the very fact of whether there is going to be a Church tomorrow.

Liturgical participation, though, should not be limited to merely taking part in the ritual. Above and beyond this outward participation, the ritual in all its forms should gradually become reflective of the people for whom it is composed; reflective of the people in their deeply rooted yearning for a brighter ray of light as they fumble their way through the adversities of life and as they seek a spiritual attachment wherefrom they hope an authority will generate that will keep their hearts orderly without rejecting them; reflective of their present-day concept of man being fundamentally good and in need not of punishment as much as of encouragement to climb higher on the ladder of personal development; reflective of the measure of their faith in man's intellectual and reasoning powers by which life has become meaningful on both the material and spiritual levels as never before; reflective of their faith that man will — in so far as God is pleased to allow — come to an unprecedented knowledge of himself for the benefit of his emotional and spiritual constitution that is now tortured by the fear of the morrow that ultimately leads to sin.

Foundational concepts and precepts such as these and others even more profound should form the substratum on which a liturgical reform — whenever it comes — should base the rationale of its theological, philosophical, and aesthetic structure. Only then, will our ritual be expressive of our Faith not only theologically but all-inclusively and pragmatically to the point of truly representing the inner fiber of the mystical body of Christ that we are as a Church.

As it is, our ritual is unnecessarily reflecting a strong theological preoccupation to the neglect or complete absence of the soul of man fighting its survival through evil and needing at this stage of its growth in the ways of God understanding and a helping hand on the part of the Church instead of minute statements of belief and a contemplation of eschatological issues.

The life hereafter is, of course, the constant concern of the Church but we should remember that one cannot seek it, or even think of it, irrespective of this temporal experience. It is the nature of this experience that will determine the quality of the life hereafter. The Orthodox teaching on the things to come — eschatology — is fully cognizant of this life as the sole and absolute determinant of the life hereafter. It is in this light that we should see and interpret the strong eschatological element that abounds in our ritual. The individual of today, we should remember, cannot understand how we can groom him for another life he cannot even visualize but leave alone to survive in this one.

Our Liturgy Cannot be Timeless Without Being Timely

Our most valued ceremonial treasure is our Liturgy, that is, the celebration of the Eucharist with the subsequent imparting to the congregation of the Body and Blood of Christ. This is our supreme act of worship by which the mystical body of Christ — the membership of the Church —

are united with the Lord not symbolically but actually and in terms of personal experience as a result of the sacred act we call Communion.

No other sacrament from among our seven sacraments is better known and more extensively shared by the Orthodox than the sacrament of Eucharist. While some of the others — such as baptism, penance, matrimony — appear to be more personal, the individual's participation in them is more or less passive, a kind of a spiritual and emotional surrendering to the authority and ritual of the Church. In the Eucharist, the Orthodox comes face to face with his personal religion on the strength of which his own grading of himself as a Christian and an Orthodox is gradually effected. His attitude toward the Eucharist and Communion reflects his adult viewpoint of himself and the degree of religious maturity he has reached in the face of the problem of being and becoming.

It is to no other sacrament that the Orthodox goes with greater measure of personal responsibility. This, on account of the extensive freedom he can exercise in interpreting the sacrament and in proceeding to receive it on the strength of his own interpretation. No amount of training on the part of the Church can generate in the believer's soul the standard attitude that the Church would wish her whole membership to entertain toward this supreme sacrament. Because the personal participation in the sacrament is so deep and so extensive, the individual member comes to realize that in the act of receiving the Body and Blood of Christ he lives his own personal and exclusive relation with God; so personal and so exclusive that associations such as those between man-woman, mother-child, appear to be shallow and colorless.

The Orthodox Communion is thus the most solitary state of personal being and yet the most self-fulfilling act of becoming, if the prerequisites to the act of Receiving are observed to the satisfaction of both the Church that dispenses the sacrament and the individual who receives it.

Consequently, the Biblical sacramental core on which the Apostolic celebration of the sacrament was based became vested with an array of theological ideas and statements to the point of our Eucharist being now — besides the supreme sacrament that it is — a dogmatical discourse of paramount importance. Our Liturgy is the first from among our ceremonial acts that acquired this kind of dogmatical significance; others did gradually follow to the extent that the most important dogmatical theses of our Church are now found in the form of beliefs expressed through prayer in our sacraments and other acts of worship.

A student with a keen eye can go through our ritual and extricate therefrom and piece together our whole dogmatical system. Our Christology, for example, is more clearly and more undoubtedly stated in our Liturgy than in any formal dogmatical statement. Also, the inaudible prayers of the priest, while the choir is singing, the liturgical hymns, are expressive of a broader interpretation of the place of the individual in the cosmos at large as well as within the Church of Christ in particular.

Hence the traditional zeal and the "defend to death" mood of Orthodox monastics in answer to any talk about liturgical reform. Hence, also, the taboo attitude of the average Orthodox and his fear to even examine his liturgical texts as he would any other literature. This kind of extreme reverential attitude has grown, in many instances, into an irrational fear of polluting the sacred were it to be examined by man's critical faculties. The "hands off our texts and ceremonies" slogan has resulted, of course, in widespread ignorance of them on the part of our people for whom, in the first place, our sacraments were gradually given their articulation.

This kind of fearful protection seems to extend even to words, sentences, and texts that are obviously mistaken in syntax and grammar, as it becomes very apparent in translation. Meanings, expressions, and words that were somehow protected in the original by virtue of being parts of the sacred whole emerge in translation stripped of their mystique and in considerable poverty of content and meaning.

Obviously, a few things require clarification. First, that which makes our Liturgy the sacrament of Eucharist is a very brief prayer on the part of the celebrant which the people do not hear and by which the priest prays to God to send down His Spirit ". . . on us and on these Gifts here offered; and make this bread the precious Body of Thy Christ; and the wine in this cup the precious Blood of Thy Christ; by changing them through the power of Thy Holy Spirit; Amen." As soon as this prayer is finished, we believe the Gifts of bread and wine to have been changed to the Body and Blood of Christ and the sacrament of Eucharist to have been completed. The consummation of the sacrament takes place through the Divine Gifts being offered to the believers in the act of Communion that follows. This is the core around which an elaborate ceremonial composition has been woven through time and in answer to the spiritual needs of contemporary congregations. It took the first five centuries of ecclesiastical life for our Liturgy to more or less stabilize in the form in which we have it today. But it would be a mistake to believe that, even at that point, it had become so rigid as not to allow subsequent changes as a result of additions, omissions, and interpolations. This is obvious even today if one witnesses our Liturgy celebrated in each of the national jurisdictions that make up the complement of the Orthodox Church here.

As the sacramental core was prologued and appended with an epilogue by other prayers and minor ceremonial acts of important symbolism, the arts that render the feeling of religion deeper and more fervent were called in and contributed to creating an elaborate performance of religious drama the equal of which the Church has yet to produce. Music crept in to express sorrow for the Cross but also joy for the Resurrection and for the individual being subsequently united through Communion with "Him who is parted but not divided, consumed but not expended." Music to express the remorse of the sinner and his hope for forgiveness, music to express the group's expectation of triumph against evil and pain within the Lord's kingdom on earth as it is in heaven. Poetry was allowed to take the spirit of the worshipper on its wings up to the heights of Olympus and down to the Castalian spring, to breathe the divinity that soared to heaven from a manger and to drink the immortality that poured out of fishermen's kyregma. Architecture was called in to provide a dome for a manger, a cross, and an empty tomb, the fruits of the love for us of God the Father.

The Eucharist became the sacrament of the adult, the supreme act of religious free choice that the individual not only could or could not exercise but could interpret in solitude, vis-a-vis himself and God, in considerable measure of personal freedom but also in an atmosphere of responsibility that would be solely his. Although the sacrament of penance was and still is prerequisite to Communion, the Orthodox feels entitled to assume personal responsibility in the eyes of God, and often presents himself to receive the Precious Gifts on the strength of his being a spiritually responsible person who could not see the reason for receiving Communion unless he believed in both the sacrament's supreme value and his imperative need for it. Perhaps, it is for this highest possible regard of the Orthodox for the Eucharist that the Last Rites of the Orthodox Church is not the sacrament of Unction but Holy Communion administered while the patient is fully conscious and properly prepared.

For the Orthodox, the concept of the Church being the mystical body of Christ fundamentally derives from the concept of the Eucharist not as a mere symbolic act of remembrance but as an invisible as well as a visible force that binds together member with member in the Communion of Christ. The individual becomes, thus, truly a member of the mystical body of Christ, a person who loses his individuality in the Grace that sustains the Church "correctly dispensing the Word of His Truth"; yet he individually grows in Christ and enjoys his divine inheritance in the spiritual solitariness to which all of us have been born.

These and many other reasons greatly contributed to the growing of our Liturgy into an institution and a work of art that people viewed as the Parthenon of Orthodoxy which could be improved no further. By the time the rest of the sacraments were given a ceremonial garment of their own and appeared as religious services proper, the Eucharist was firmly established in the conscience of the Church as the one sacrament in the life of the adult Orthodox with no equal in theological importance, personal significance, and in its tutoring the individual into the bold religious metaphysics of Orthodox theosis.

Aesthetically, the mind and heart of the Orthodox had spoken *de profundis* while composing the Liturgy, and little or nothing could be said or acted that would add further significance in meaning or could deepen the sacrament's beauty. The Byzantine Liturgy is, indeed, a hard to relate experience, as deep and extensive as the worshipper would allow to himself, conditioned only by one's spontaneity in feeling and by his preparedness to let the performance usher his mind and heart to a world where matter and mind come to a knowledge of each other that proves utterly unique and personally gratifying to the individual.

Hence, the deeply rooted conviction of the average Orthodox clergyman and layman, that the Liturgy is perfect, it is timeless. It is above time and conditions, peoples and civilizations, cultures, socio-economic changes, scientific and technological advances. It is even above and beyond advances in man's understanding of mental and spiritual realities that make up the continuum of our present experience in the midst of a personal and group life that bears little or no relation to personal and community living at the time our Liturgy was formulated.

People are right when they claim that the Liturgy is timeless and above the transitory character and temporariness of human development on this earth. But as to which part of its articulation and form? Obviously, only as regards its sacramental core, the Epiclesis with the act of consecration. This is the truly eternal element in our Liturgy, the one from which salvation generates, the act of uniting the temporal man with the eternal Christ.

This, because irrespective of man's development and irrespective of the type of personal experience to which he is at times subjected, his inner problems remain the same and his inner search for a principle of spiritual origin and authority to which he can refer his whole existence is now as pressing as ever before. This means that our need for Christ has not diminished, on the contrary, the more we advance in the knowledge of ourselves the more our inner vacuum grows if this knowledge is not oriented toward a Christological understanding of being and becoming.

For us, the Eucharist is a very tangible means of entering a new era of personal becoming, it is a source of strength — and if one's faith is sufficiently strong — a source of personal strength that can counterbalance in us the duress of material living and its promptings to spiritual nihilism. For those who believe Christ to be present in the Eucharist, Holy Communion not only provides replenishment to one's consumed spirituality in the strife of personal relationships, but, above all, it generates a power that comes gradually to prevent our loss of spirituality. Obviously, true weariness of human living does not result from bodily aging but from the wearing out of one's inner strength as a result of his spiritual deposits becoming depleted.

But the Liturgy cannot be timeless without being timely as well. Our predecessors provided a liturgical garment for the Eucharistic sacramental core that proved to be perfect

143

for ministering to the particular needs of the Church and her membership at the time. The synthesis, interests, occupations, education, personal and group objectives, together with the particular viewing of our Church's congregation of life in general, are all reflected in our hymns and priestly prayers that make up the Liturgy. When the liturgical Fathers of our Church put the finishing touches on the ceremonial garment of the Eucharist, they had completed a most artful portrayal of man and his soul in search of personal redemption at a particular point of history and under certain social and national conditions.

The Liturgy as the Church's supreme act of worship emerged not only as a work of art but as a true to reality drama of contemporary Christians seeking the timeless and eternal Christ. As such, our Liturgy proved to contemporary congregations to be not only timeless but timely as well, that is, relevant to their intellectual, moral, and emotional frames of understanding and behavior.

That is precisely what today's congregations want for themselves, too. They want the timelessness of our Liturgy to be given a timely garment, a context that derives from today's experience, from today's nature of intellectual pursuits, and from today's moral appraisal of personal relationships in the face of the present inward and outward division in our social environment at large. For, though the moral constitution of man is still plagued by the same diseases as of old, his moral understanding of the world has suffered changes and his attitude toward disciplines that deal with his welfare — including religion — has become more demanding but potentially more rewarding if he is convinced as to their desirability and effectiveness.

Our need for God has not lessened; if anything, it has deepened as our mental acuity is reaching its full potentials and has, as a result, seeded our emotional self with charges that can set afire the whole world by a push-button kind of war. Our personal relationships, even within one's most immediate circle, have taken a tone and a depth undreamed of at the time our Liturgy was composed. They are not straightforward anymore, because they are not controlled by spiritual leaderships that every one would be willing to succumb to. As a high level education has become commonplace, and as personal toil is in demand and is amply rewarded, personal independence from want has created countless free people but has also created countless new inward problems for them. The individual who by necessity had in the past to belong to someone or to something is left now on his own, and his thus resulting spiritual freedom has generated in his heart and soul a fearful solitariness and a very uncertain spiritual morrow for him.

It is the strenuous contention of this writer that if we leave this new breed of free men spiritually unguided by presenting them with a kind of religious experience that would fail to murmur to their inner ears the hope of looking upward and the certainty of being seen and watched from up there, their search for meaning could just as well lead them to an understanding of reality solely on the basis of the tangible and enjoyable.

From whichever angle we may view our spiritual situation at this time, current demands for meaning and relevancy are not the passing fancy of a youth who have everything and want to try everything. It is the affliction and the blessing of having reached a degree of control over

145

nature and ourselves that finally have brought us face to face with the fundamental issues of being and becoming. We have done and we are doing exceedingly well with improving, modifying, or even completely changing conditions that can exercise an influence on our physical existence. But by so doing, our relations with God have changed in emphasis; our liturgical petitions for God's help regarding conditions and forces that could control our livelihood are not meaningful any more.

The Liturgical Commissions and Committees that began to come into being in Europe and here will receive their first shock by being confronted with the question of the legitimacy and validity of the stress of our liturgical dialogue with God on outward and temporal conditions. Of course, the concern for the temporal in our Liturgy makes the congregation's offering to God all the more complete and wholesome, but this type of concern appears to be irrelevant to today's congregations.

We are not concerned today with the needs and wants of a predominantly agrarian Orthodox congregation. Even if we were, we do not pray for weather anymore because we can practically make it to our specifications. We do not pray for crops to succeed; we use our chemistry to fortify plants and destroy their predators. We do not pray for rain; we can make it. If we can't, we do not raise crops in that particular climate, and so on. Our control over natural environment is, indeed, astonishing, but this should not make us insolent. If we do not have to pray for favorable weather anymore, we have to pray harder for the human mind and man's moral constitution that are both responsible for bringing us where we are now and where we are headed for the future.

All this means that our need for God is now greater and deeper considering that we are concerned more with intangibles than with tangibles. Therefore, our whole orientation toward the divine needs to be realigned so as to express our real spiritual wants. The changes we will be forced to effect so as to make our Liturgy the epitome of our lives and of the whole spectrum of our present-day religious orientation should not change either the purpose or the spiritual breadth of this cardinal act of the experience of being Orthodox. The timelessness of our Liturgy will be found only through pursuing its timeliness reflected in the Church's way of thinking, feeling, and living.

INDEX